EXPRESSIVE TYPE

Quarto is the authority on a wide range of topics.

Quarto educates, entertains and enriches the lives of our readers—enthusiasts and lovers of hands-on living.

www.QuartoKnows.com

© 2017 Quarto Publishing Group USA Inc.

First published in the United States of America in 2017 by Rockport Publishers, an imprint of Quarto Publishing Group USA Inc.
100 Cummings Center
Suite 265-D
Beverly, Massachusetts 01915-6101
Telephone: (978) 282-9590
Fax: (978) 283-2742
QuartoKnows.com
Visit our blogs at QuartoKnows.com

MIX
Paper from responsible sources
FSC® C104723

10 9 8 7 6 5 4 3 2 1

ISBN: 978-1-63159-273-7

Library of Congress Cataloging-in-Publication Data available.

Design: Paul Burgess at Burge Agency
Cover Image: Alex Fowkes
Photography: All photography by the individual designers except page 24, Brian Samuels and Brett Warren; page 25, Brett Warren and Michael Tucker; page 38, Kathryn Kelly DeWitt; page 39, Christian Helms; page 42, Neumeister & NINE; page 50, Shane Cranford and Ross Clodfelter; page 52, Margherita Porra; page 58, creative and art direction, Jovan Tkulja, design and illustrations, Marijana Rot; page 92, Brigida González; page 104, interior design by Lauren Shaw, photography by Lauren Kallen; page 108, Alex Wallace; page 111, Sean Carabarin.

Printed in China

ALEX FOWKES

UNIQUE TYPOGRAPHIC

· DESIGN ·

EXPRESSIVE TYPE

· IN SKETCHBOOKS ·

IN PRINT & ON LOCATION

AROUND THE GLOBE

ROCKPORT

CONTENTS

INTRODUCTION   6

CATEGORY 1   8
BRANDING

JON CONTINO   10
MARTIN SCHMETZER   14
NEIGHBORHOOD STUDIO   16
TOBIAS HALL   18
ALAN CHEETHAM   20
OAT   22
PECK & COMPANY   24
ALLAN PETERS   26
POL SOLSANA   28
BMD DESIGN   30
AURELIE MARON   34
GONZALO LEBERO   36
LAUREN DICKENS   38
KENDRICK KIDD   40
LACHLAN BULLOCK   42

CATEGORY 2   44
PACKAGING

YANI & GUILLE   46
DEVICE   50
ARITHMETIC   52
JAMIE CLARKE TYPE   54
KELLY THOMPSON   56
PETER GREGSON STUDIO   58
SAM LEE   60
BRANDWAGON   62
CHAD MICHAEL STUDIO   64
THE SHALLOW TREE   68
TOM LANE   70
REYNOLDS AND REYNER   72
SNASK   74
SPASM   76
VAULT49   78

CATEGORY 3   80

ENVIRONMENTAL

GEMMA O'BRIEN	82
ASHLEY WILLERTON	86
BRYAN PATRICK TODD	88
SHED DESIGN	90
BÜRO UEBELE VISUELLE KOMMUNIKATION	92
ADAM VICAREL	94
BEN JOHNSTON	96
ANDREAS M HANSEN	100
CRAIG BLACK	102
JEREMIAH BRITTON	104
JOEL BIRCH	106
LILLY LOU	108
DIRTY BANDITS	110
NO ENTRY DESIGN	112
GED PALMER	114

CATEGORY 4   116

SELF-INITIATED

LAUREN HOM	118
CHRIS PIASCIK	122
CARL FREDRIK ANGELL, A.K.A. FRISSO	124
JAMES LEWIS	126
WASTE STUDIO	128
MARTINA FLOR	130
ROB DRAPER	132
DARREN BOOTH	136
BOHIE PALECEK	138
IAN BARNARD	140
JUSTIN POULTER	142
SARA MARSHALL	144
BOBBY HAIQALSYAH	146
LUKE LUCAS	148
VELVET SPECTRUM	150

CATEGORY 5   152

REAL-WORLD BRIEFS

BRANDING BRIEF	154
PACKAGING BRIEF	155
ENVIRONMENTAL BRIEF	156
SELF-INITIATED BRIEF	157

ACKNOWLEDGMENTS	158
ABOUT THE AUTHOR	159

INTRODUCTION

Expressive Type is a collection of work and wisdom from sixty designers, typographers, and artists from around the world, all of whom have different styles and approaches to the way they work. Everyone has a signature style—whether it is hand-drawn type, interesting detailing, or just a unique idea. All the work shown here caught my eye for a particular reason. I did not want to represent only typographers in the book; I included designers and artists, too, from different backgrounds, whose various influences make their projects more interesting.

Expressive Type is organized into categories based on medium. The first category, branding, looks at successful logos and brand identity projects. Here, I convey the particular elements or individuality about a project. Following these, we see how the logo is applied within the branding, materials, and stationery. Category 2, packaging, looks at quirky and alluring boxes, labels, bottles, and more. Whether making use of varying materials, print techniques, or eye-catching designs, these projects are all inspirational in their variety when faced with similar parameters. Category 3, environmental, shows work and pieces from around the world, demonstrating how typography and artwork can change the feel of a space,

express important messages to customers or employees, and, in general, make the environment a more enjoyable place to be. The final category, self-initiated, looks at the personal work of designers, typographers, and artists—the personal projects they do when not working for clients that help advance their own practice and notoriety in the design world.

I have always been a huge fan of the behind-the-scenes processes of a project. Although it wasn't feasible to fully document the process behind every project, I include insider information on how various projects were created, what materials were used, and what problems were encountered. You'll also see process shots, which I always find

interesting. Every contributor has provided project descriptions that add another layer of understanding to the work.

With *Expressive Type*, I've added an extra element that might inspire you to try something new. The final category in the book, real-world briefs, contains a brief based on each category presented in the book: branding, packaging, environmental, and self-initiated. Each strives to be as close to an actual brief that designers would receive from a client. The idea behind these projects is to inspire, guide, and compel you to try something new and create something fun.

Branding comes in many shapes and sizes. The very notion of being able to represent a company's ethos, values, and target market in just one identity is not an easy task. There are many more elements to consider: the logo application in different places all the way down to the paper stock used. Every aspect is carefully considered and designed to affect particular feelings and emotions with viewers and customers. Many of the projects displayed in this section have been through multiple versions and countless revisions so everything is just right.

CATEGORY 1

BRANDING

JON CONTINO	10
MARTIN SCHMETZER	14
NEIGHBORHOOD STUDIO	16
TOBIAS HALL	18
ALAN CHEETHAM	20
OAT	22
PECK & COMPANY	24
ALLAN PETERS	26
POL SOLSANA	28
BMD DESIGN	30
AURELIE MARON	34
GONZALO LEBERO	36
LAUREN DICKENS	38
KENDRICK KIDD	40
LACHLAN BULLOCK	42

AMERICAN

Cycles

BIKES & PARTS

JON CONTINO

New York native Jon Contino is at the forefront of today's most influential designers. His unique stylistic approach blends Old World whimsy with a modern, minimalistic sensibility that creates a distinct personality imitated time and again. Jon's dedicated efforts continue to blur boundaries and affect modern trends in all facets of the creative industry.

Jon has received numerous accolades for his fusion of Old and New World aesthetics and continues to garner the attention of media outlets, as well as large-scale agencies. Jon resides in New York with his wife, Erin, and daughter, Fiona, where he operates a full-time studio and works as creative director for The Hidden Sea, brand manager for Past Lives, and creative director of an apparel and accessories brand bearing his name.

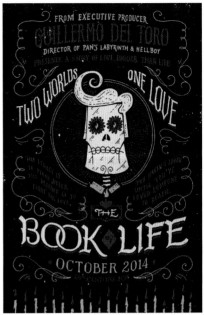

THE BOOK OF LIFE

Coming into this project, I expected the typical "too many cooks in the kitchen" routine. After all, 20th Century Fox isn't exactly a start-up. Creative Director Neri Rivas called me one afternoon as I was driving down the West Side Highway in Manhattan and asked if I'd be interested in working on a new animated feature film by Guillermo del Toro with a Mexican Day-of-the-Dead theme. At that point, I didn't care what he had to say next; I was sold.

One of the best parts of the process was digging deep into Mexican culture and lore. I've always been really intrigued with the creative history of Mexico, so having the chance to put my own spin on it was an amazing opportunity. The lettering, the iconography, the stories. So much to absorb and build upon.

In terms of the actual process, we didn't really reinvent the wheel. Neri and I traded sketches back and forth until we came up with a collection of ideas that made sense with the script and the characters, as a whole. Then it was a race to execute.

We spent well over a year developing an entire campaign of logos, posters, merchandise, and even a font, to be ready for the film's opening. By the time we finished, it felt like we had built a skyscraper. You don't realize how much goes into branding and marketing a film like this until you understand how many deliverables you actually need to go live with. I'll never forget the day I saw everything come to life with the first trailer. I can only compare it to the day my daughter was born. It was exhilarating.

THE HIDDEN SEA

The Hidden Sea is a wine that was made at a very special vineyard. Limestone Coast Vineyard off the southern coast of Australia is in an area where numerous sinkholes opened up, revealing a series of caves beneath the growing grapes. One of those caves contained a whale fossil—completely preserved in its ceiling—that actually formed the perfect filtration system for the wine grapes to thrive. To represent this, we created a simple script lettering piece with an intertwined whale illustration, which became the basis for an entire narrative that would expand to create a full-scale folklore.

Most wine companies are focused on how the product sits on the shelves; we were more concerned with developing a cult following for the brand. We looked at companies, such as Apple, that put design first and don't worry about appealing to the masses. "If you build it, they will come." I've always felt that when you design something to try to please everyone, it loses any sense of personality and winds up appealing to no one. But if you find a niche and exploit it, you can appeal to a group of people that will live and die with the brand. Eventually the masses will come around, but it's more about developing that core following before anything else.

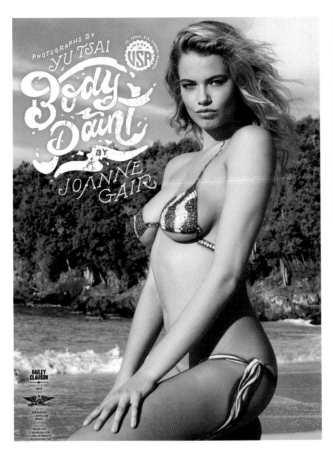

SPORTS ILLUSTRATED
SWIMSUIT ISSUE 2015

It's not every day that you're asked to rebrand an American icon. The task was to take *Sports Illustrated* in a different direction for 2015 and do something it had never done before: create an entire brand language to accompany one of the most-talked-about issues in recent memory.

Chris, the creative director, kept things tight. He is the type of person who makes our jobs so easy. He and I went back and forth with concepts, trading ideas and ways to make things bigger and better than ever before. He wanted to be involved in everything to ensure the quality was kept as high as possible, which I greatly appreciated.

When it comes down to it, though, this was a project just like any other. I always take each new project as seriously as the previous one. Whether the work is being seen by seventy people or seventy million people, it's humbling to know that once the excitement ends, you're back to square one. This project reminds me that if I'm ever given the opportunity again to make something that could affect a large number of people, it needs to be done efficiently and in a memorable way, because even a project this big will be replaced after a year. Make it count.

MARTIN SCHMETZER

Martin Schmetzer is a Stockholm-based designer specializing in hand-drawn typography with a high level of detail and diligence. As part of Rithuset, Sweden's most renowned illustration agency, he works alongside multidisciplinary artists of varying styles. His day to day consists of designing logotypes, packaging, custom typography, and illustrations.

In the mid-nineties, Martin first came in contact with hand-drawn typography— through graffiti. Graffiti was a good way for him to explore the alphabet and learn how the letters are put together. As a graffiti writer you don't have to follow any rules and you can twist and bend the letters until you tame the words into something uniquely your own.

As a graffiti writer he often aimed for symmetry in his pieces, something that follows Martin to this day in his logotypes and illustrations. His style has evolved through many years of development, but you can still see a hint of the graffiti background in most of his designs. What he loves most about lettering is the interaction hand-drawn typography can have to the meaning of a word, and how the letters next to each other play together and shape an integrality.

BUTCHER'S PLATE

Martin was commissioned and art directed by Retail United to design a logotype and pattern design for Sibylla's new sausage concept Butcher's Plate. The task was to develop a handcrafted design inspired by the English gastro-pub culture, that reflects the premium craftsmanship and high-quality ingredients that go into their sausages and side orders.

NEIGHBORHOOD STUDIO

A graduate of Portfolio Center in Atlanta, Curtis Jinkins began his professional career at Planet Propaganda in Madison, Wisconsin. Four years later, he moved back to his native Texas where he spent several drudgery-filled years at an advertising agency. Curtis established his own graphic design studio, Neighborhood Studio, in late 2009 in the hill country of central Texas, outside Austin.

BANGERS

Work for Banger's Sausage House and Beer Garden began in 2010. From the ground up, Neighborhood Studio had a hand in every aspect of the initial stages of development—concept, atmosphere, name, signage, logo, menus, waitstaff apparel, and murals. Essentially the project was every graphic design student's senior thesis. Work for Banger's is ongoing as the project expands into consumer packaged goods, and the purchase of an adjacent lot brings new opportunities for signage, wayfinding systems, murals, and so on.

Bell & Oak

DENTON TEXAS

BELL & OAK

Bell & Oak is Clint Wilkinson's leather goods shop, occupying the same spot where his grandfather has been hand-tooling leather saddles since the 1950s. The name Bell & Oak comes from the street corner where the shop is located in Denton, Texas, and from certain common themes in leather tooling—oak leaves and bells. Leather stamps used on soft leather create incredible impressions—definitely an honor to add branding to heritage and craft.

TOBIAS HALL

Tobias Hall is a freelance illustrator, letterer, designer, and mural artist working out of London. He graduated in 2010 from Coventry University with a degree in illustration and animation. Having initially started as a conceptual illustrator, Tobias began working with typography and lettering soon after graduating and hasn't looked back since. He prides himself on his versatility and his ability to work in any given type style. When he's not writing in the third person, Tobias likes to draw things inspired by the music he listens to or things he reads.

KITTEL'S

I start by sketching a series of compositional roughs until I settle on one that I think achieves the best balance for the project. Then I begin a larger-scale rough—drawing all lines by hand, initially in pencil, before scanning them into Adobe Photoshop, where I'll make any corrections with kerning, alignment, and the like. After that, I print out those pencil lines at a low opacity and start working in "neat" with pigment liners of varying weights to create a final version. The reason I work this way is that scanning the pencil lines not only gives me a chance to correct any mistakes, but it also means that, when it comes to scanning those neat pen lines again, I get a cleaner scan (as opposed to also scanning any original pencil lines I've not rubbed out properly).

Once I've scanned the neat pen lines, it becomes a case of coloring and texturing the work in Photoshop. Occasionally I'll use a Wacom tablet for the coloring but, most of the time, it's fairly crudely done by using the pen tool and filling areas with the paint bucket tool. I also scan bits of paper and use the soft light layer setting in Photoshop to create textures.

For the Kittel's project, I was contacted by a man setting up a shop in Hamburg, Germany, which was to specialize in various high-quality British goods. He planned on stocking a lot of different items, so one of the challenges was communicating all the different product lines succinctly within one logo crest. I started by creating some fairly polished roughs, one of which he chose to develop. Then it was a case of refining that chosen rough.

That process took a fairly long time and there were a lot of amends before we finally settled on the finished piece. I think it was worth it, though; I'm happy with how the suite turned out. Many people have asked me about the relevance of the peacock. The reason is because that's what the client requested—I'm still not sure why!

ALAN CHEETHAM

Hailing from the county of Derbyshire, England, by day, Alan works as a creative designer at Subism, a small creative and digital-based studio set back in the city center of Derby. By night, he tries to stay creative, usually experimenting with custom type and his never-ending obsession with hand lettering. This keeps his creative finger on the design pulse and away from all the other drab stuff in life, such as politics, crappy memes, GIFs of cats, and relentless images of the avocado.

GREAT SCOTT CO.

The great explorer Robert Falcon Scott inspired the look and feel of this brand. "Scott of the Antarctic," a naval captain, died while attempting to be the first person to reach the South Pole during the early 1900s. On the notion of great exploration and the historical value of Captain Robert Falcon Scott, the identity "Great Scott Co." surfaced.

Unfortunately the concept and brand was left dormant in cyber space. Initially, it was going to be a brand that sold quirky, stylish quality lifestyle products made by designers for designers.

The Great Scott Co. wording was fully customized based on referencing two of my favorite sans serif fonts: "Ginger" by Rick Banks and "Acrom" by The Northern Block type foundry, creating a suitable hybrid. As the main mark, I incorporated a zeppelin illustration to reflect an essence of exploring the great unknown. As an additional touch, I customized the letter A to look like the point of a compass to signify the exploration theme further.

EST. 2014

GREAT SCOTT Co

QUALITY LIFESTYLE PRODUCTS

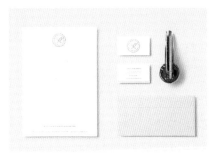

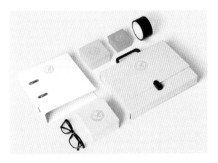

ROBERT CAINS DECORATORS

Robert Cains Decorators is a bespoke interior and exterior decorating company based in the county of Derbyshire, UK. Thirty-two years after the family-run business was established in 1984, the brand identity was in desperate need of a modern refresh. The logo mark drew design references from old Victorian illustrations that adopt extraordinarily fine hatch-line details. So as not to complicate the logo mark with vast amounts of line detail, I kept the design clean and simple by using just enough detail to give the entire logo design clarity, with plenty of depth for viewing at smaller sizes.

A modest nod toward Victorian-style illustrations helped the overall visual tone of the identity reflect on its traditional roots of fine craftsmanship. To complement the brand refresh further, new stationery items were introduced with soft pastel colors and gold foiling for an added touch of class.

ROBERT CAINS

DECORATORS

OAT

Oat builds brands through the alchemy of ideas and narrative truth. A sound brand strategy uncovers the intangible values that inform consumer perception. This approach results in a brand narrative that is the foundation of internal operations and external communication.

Jennifer Lucey-Brzoza is an internationally recognized designer. Born and raised in Boston, she studied fine art at the School of the Museum of Fine Arts, Boston, with a concentration in photography and drawing.

Rory Keohane, also a Boston native, is a brand strategist and entrepreneur. He studied literature at Oberlin College in Ohio. The couple lives and works in Somerville, Massachusetts, where, together, they run Oat.

ISLAND CREEK OYSTERS

Island Creek Oysters is a place where salt-of-the-earth farmers live by the tide. As a nationally beloved brand, the soul of Island Creek Oysters is embodied by a true sense of place. The comprehensive brand expression focuses on people and texture, balancing the rough-and-tumble nature of life by the shore with the refined elegance of their product.

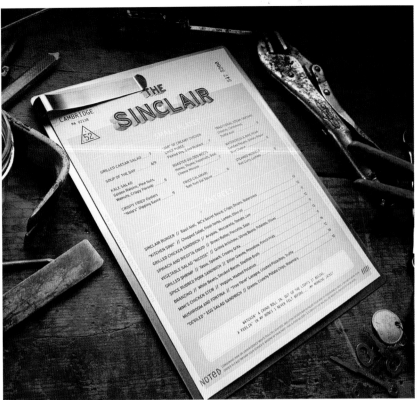

THE SINCLAIR

The Sinclair declares its industrial style by setting the stage with single-stroke neon and channel lettering. The collateral design captures the rugged pragmatism of a workshop and the clean lines of a factory back office. An editable area for lyrics and quotes strengthens the relationship between the restaurant and the music hall, weaving in elements from touring bands.

PECK & COMPANY

Peck & Company opened in 2004 in Nashville and has offered brand identity and package design services for a wide range of clients in an ever-growing number of industries. With a healthy dose of hard knocks and cunning wit, we bring interesting brands to life. During the past twelve-plus years, Peck & Company has built relationships with clients across the Unites States and abroad, inspired by the people behind the brands whose stories we are fortunate enough to tell.

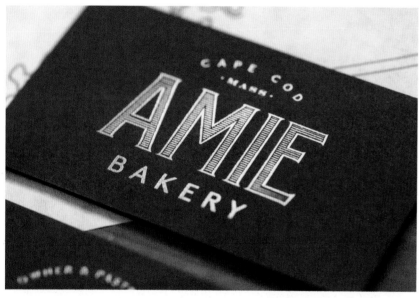

AMIE BAKERY

Amie is a small specialty bakery on Cape Cod, Massachusetts, that likes to think of itself as the town's kitchen. Named after its owner and chef, Amie Smith, whose first name translates to "friend" in French, the Amie Bakery brand needed to communicate the warm and inviting nature of home. Inspired by beautiful, ornate vintage baking tins and Victorian engraved type styles of the period, our challenge was achieving the delicate balance of sophistication and comfort. We wanted to create a brand that was equally memorable and classic as this bygone time that meant so much to Amie. Through the creation of custom patterns, custom logotype, and a wide range of type-driven illustrations, we created a brand that has the flexibility to be executed in any medium, while still maintaining consistency.

MERCER SUPPLY CO.

BARBER / SALON

MERCER SUPPLY CO.

Mercer Supply Co. is a modern barbershop and mercantile for those weekend rabble-rousers with a weekday reputation to uphold. In the capital city and college town of Baton Rouge, the clientele can vary greatly from one appointment to the next—but one thing everyone has in common is attitude. The Mercer clientele are not afraid to go at it alone, but they also understand the value of good friends and strategic relationships.

Like the Mercer clientele, pelicans are gregarious birds that live communally but often hunt and feed alone. But pelicans, much like Southern gentlemen, make great friends and awful pets. So this south Louisiana brand—built on the contrast of refinement and rebellion—required sharp skills and steady hands to tame and translate the disparity. Through copywriting, photography, custom patterns, and varied printing techniques, Mercer Supply Co. draws the distinction between being a gentleman and just being gentle. We wanted to create a brand that was bold at times, refined at others, and always up for a good time.

ALLAN PETERS

Allan Peters is a creative director and designer from Minneapolis. His work has been recognized by every major design publication, and *Graphic Design USA* named him a person to watch in 2013. Allan runs Peters Design Company (PDCo), which has worked with clients ranging from Nike to ESPN to Amazon. He has also started the badge hunting movement, not only in the Midwest but across the country. Allan participates in numerous talks within the design community and has a great influence on many designers.

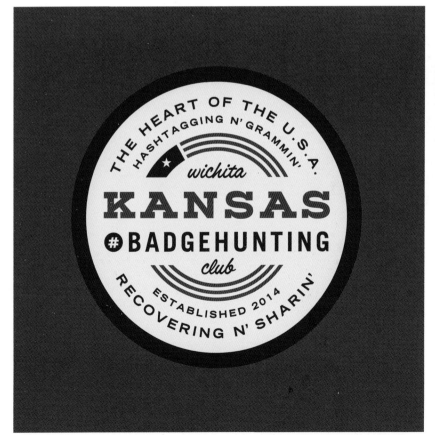

BADGE HUNTING

One of the main issues with current design is that people find their inspiration from other current work. Design work these days is made quickly and it can be difficult for nondesigners to tell the difference between well-crafted work and work that was cranked out in a few hours with little to no thought, strategy, or visual history. Before computers, design took time. Designers were craftsmen. If you have to place each piece of type by hand, you're forced to get into the details. Revisions took weeks versus the one- to two-day turnaround deadlines clients expect now. Rather than searching Pinterest, dribble, or found, I dig up work from the past that was made with craft—work made with time; work that was respected.

I find trends that are lost in obscurity and I try to learn from that work. I document anything I find inspiring. Many designers do this same kind of thing. It's the idea that we dig to seek inspiration. We look in old broken-down shacks, in tumbledown barns, or in your grandpa's tool shed. Most of that stuff will end up in a dumpster one day. We try to save it by documenting it with photography. What makes #BadgeHunting different is that I share it all with the world. I make it accessible to all designers and I encourage them to do the same. I don't expect to make a dollar doing it. I just want to make this classic work available to every designer so it helps move our visual culture forward by learning from the past.

POL SOLSONA

Pol Solsona is an independent graphic designer and art director based in Barcelona who works with national and international clients across multiple disciplines. He has lived in Barcelona, Helsinki, and New York, working with the biggest advertising agencies in Finland and well-known international designers, such as Stefan Sagmeister and Jessica Walsh. Having worked with twenty different nationalities has given him a worldwide vision of the design culture and its creative thinking.

With more than ten years of experience working in advertising and graphic design studios, his main focus is on visual identities, eye-catching images, and web design. With an obsessive attention to detail and wide knowledge of techniques and disciplines, his network of national and international collaborators ensures unique solutions for each project, with functionality and user experience as main points of the process. His work stands out with its own voice, always looking for a personality that escapes from the topics, empowering the client's position in the market.

CINEMAISSÍ

The Helsinki Latin American Film Festival celebrated its eleventh edition in 2016. Cinemaissí has become the most important Scandinavian independent festival introducing updated films by new talents and well-known worldwide directors from Latin American countries.

The festival needed an upgrade that would support the curation and quality of the film selection and, at the same time, connect with the Finnish target audience without losing its Latin American spirit.

I came up with a modular system of simple lines of color against a dark backdrop— a wave-like form that derives from "an abstraction of popcorn," as well as the outlines of Finnish designer Alvar Aalto's iconic designs, including his Savoy Vase. The contrast between the lines, backdrop, and type evokes the same feeling you experience while being at the festival: a combination of the happy liveliness of the Latin countries against the dark and gloomy Finnish backdrop.

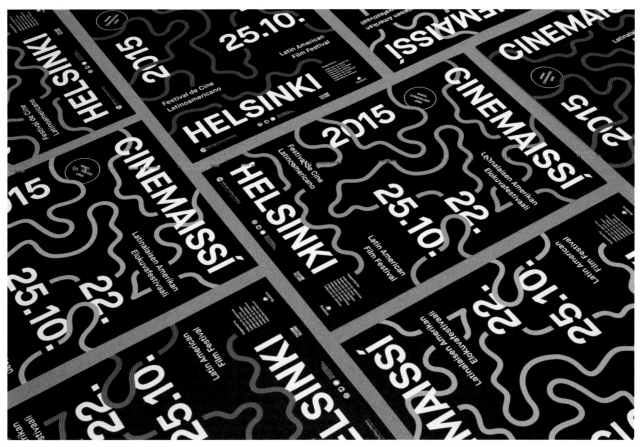

BMD DESIGN

The clatter of machinery is heard, the smell of gasoline enters our nostrils, the letters dance and stretch, slips of black or blue ink, drawn by expert hands. The work of BMD projects us into France in the 1930s. Yet behind these three letters hides Bruno Michaud, who created his Bordeaux studio in early 2001. A graphic designer in the early 1990s in Toulouse, Bruno has retained a love for craftsmanship—the one before the computer. Rotring pens, pencil, cutter, glue, brush, roughs ... working by hand takes more time, but it allows him to be one with what he creates and stimulates all his senses.

Today, "handmade" creates a craze and many brands are turning to its values: authenticity, expertise, back to the roots, craft, and secure. In a society in crisis marked by individualism and frantic rhythms, the handmade humanizes, as a supplement to the soul. Logos, fonts, pictograms: Bruno makes and remakes, traces, erases, and inks, always pushing farther in his search for graphic references. To feed his visual vocabulary, he scours the French archives—a wealth of typographic heritage. These are his main sources of inspiration.

His designs look at industrial archives unearthed in flea markets and libraries. Constantly on the lookout for typographic signs or clues, he lists and categorizes them. It is then, through the hand, he is inspired by them.

KOOPER FAMILY WHISKEY CO.

Kooper Family Whiskey is a single-barrel American whiskey made in very small batches. It is located in the very progressive city of Austin, Texas, where it has strong local support and demand for handcrafted, organic, locally made products.

The business is 100 percent family owned and operated. The Kooper brand needed typography and graphic craftsmanship—something also subtly alchemical—which makes it such a great fit for the whiskey. Kooper also wants to make t-shirts and other merchandise with alternate logos.

TANK GARAGE WINERY

Tank Garage Winery is a small micro winery housed in a renovated, 1930s art deco-style gas station in the rugged outpost of Calistoga, California. The front bays of the original garage highlight the Tank Garage Winery and tasting room that features iconic, inspired, crafted, and authentic items related to winemaking, surfing, motorcycles, "automobilia," and all things vintage and California cool. The wines of Tank Garage feature art-driven, one-off art, and historic images that will become desired and collected.

The winemaking is all done by hand by the owner in case lots of 150 cases or fewer. We needed to establish an authentic crafted logo to match.

JPR CYCLES

JPR is a French motorcycle customizer, specializing in the Harley-Davidson brand. It was established in Bordeaux, and for more than twenty years has been preparing motorcycles in its workshop (atelier). JPR custom manufactures individual parts, offering true craftsmanship. JPR wanted me to create two logos that would establish and affirm its passion, authenticity, craft work, and extensive experience in the business of motorcycle customization.

WELCOMING Committee

 Amber Ale EasyChair

KOMODO DRAGONFLY BLACK IPA

WheatAle

COASTBUSTER IMPERIAL IPA

BREWER'S CHOICE

BAD Elmer's PORTER

UPLAND BREWING CO.

HARVEST ALE

OHTOBERFEST BAVARIAN

Campside SESSION IPA

DRAGONFLY IPA

LATITUDE Adjustment

MARION the the AGRARIAN DRY HOPPED FARMHOUSE ALE

HELIOS PALE ALE

UPLAND BRANDING CAMPAIGN

The rebranding campaign here is extensive, beginning with a new logo and branching out to include new packaging for eight of Upland's most popular beers. The goal was simple: capture the quality, culture, and spirit that make Upland and its community unique.

The handcrafted nature of the beer is reflected in the extensive use of hand-lettered type and illustrations, whether in the distinctive hills logo or in the packaging and related materials. The personality of the company, meanwhile, comes through in the description of each beer that accompanies the illustrations.

AURELIE MARON

Born in New Caledonia with a French background, Aurelie Maron moved to Australia in 2010 to study at Griffith University for her bachelor's degree in digital media. After working for two major design studios in the city of Gold Coast, she decided to work as a freelancer. A year later, she opened her first design studio in Gold Coast.

Aurelie has always been passionate about typography, even though she did not know it was a real discipline taught in universities. In 2012, one of her university projects was to illustrate a typographic quote on a blackboard using chalk. After publishing the project online, she received hundreds of emails from people asking for more commissioned work. Since then, Aurelie has been busy creating many typographic pieces.

TYPISM LOGOTYPE

Typism is the brainchild of "tactile typographer" and lecturer Dominique Falla. In 2013 I was asked to participate in the design conference, Typism, as a guest speaker and as the designer of the Typism logotype. The one-day conference was held in Pacific Fair in Gold Coast, and all the speakers came together to talk about their typographic work. It was the first creative conference in Australia to focus exclusively on the craft of typography.

Obviously, the work I did for this project was quite challenging. I had to create a typographic logo that would appeal to all the type lovers while remaining attractive and easy to read to attract a broader audience. I decided to use a cursive custom typeface and added symmetrical flourishes to make the logo even more elegant. The process involved hours of sketching on paper and refining the vector artwork on the computer.

KINETIC CAFÉ

After creating more than six concepts for the client using six different names, it was finally decided that the new café located in the Gold Coast suburbs would be called Kinetic Café. The interior of the café had a retro cycling theme. My client wanted the logo to be hand drawn with chalk to give it a more authentic look.

Once the vector version of the logo was done, it was then applied to other media, such as loyalty cards, paper towels, aprons, stationery and so on. The use of dark brown in the branding not only complements the vintage theme, but it also reminds us of the color of coffee, which emphasizes the warm and comfy feel of the place.

GONZALO LEBRERO

Born in Santander, a city in northern Spain, Gonzalo started his creative development drawing in schoolbooks and on class tables. He grew up influenced by graffiti and began painting on the streets, where he took inspiration from urban art. Gonzalo loved designing letters and murals with friends and, at the age of twenty-four, he started working for Ogilvy as an art director managing big brands, such as American Express, BMW, IBM, Movistar, Guggenheim, and Renault. After four years at Ogilvy, he focused on freelancing and moved to New York City for three months, which greatly influenced his design. Once Gonzalo returned, he opened his own design studio in Madrid, specializing in vintage lettering, branding, and digital projects, creating inspirational work and creative concepts.

LIVES AND LEVELS

Based in Sheffield, UK, Lives and Levels is a skateboard clothing company established in 2012 by brothers Tom and Oli Sykes.

I have loved and practiced the sport of skateboarding since I was young. So when I was asked to design some lettering logos for this urban, independent skateboard brand I was excited.

As always, I started designing sketches with pencil and paper and then worked on the computer with Adobe Illustrator and my Wacom tablet. I designed the letters with a thin, continuous line, similar to when I made graffiti in the past. I also used familiar techniques such as shading in some versions.

VALENTINA KOSTINA

Valentina Kostina is a Russian natural cosmetics company. I was asked to develop the logo design with just two requirements: create a vintage style and include the Pisces zodiac sign in the logo. I started the process drawing some sketches with pencil. I thought it was a good idea to design soft letters, like the effect produced by natural cosmetics on the skin, using a fine and regular stroke.

To give an organic and vintage touch, I added texture, an effect I often rely on to create my logos. To create the Pisces zodiac sign, I thought about adding different design elements and drew a horizontal arrow that connects the two sides of the sign.

LAUREN DICKENS

Lauren Dickens is a designer, artist, and typographer based in Austin, Texas. After earning her BFA in design from The University of Texas at Austin in 2011, she got a pretty good gig as a designer at Helms Workshop, a strategic branding studio. She freelances and pursues personal work in her free time when not wrangling dogs. Being a native Texan, she's drawn to a minimal yet meaningful aesthetic and strives to create things that feel purposeful, with clever quirks that add a bit of wit to the work.

KKDW

This project was close to my heart because the client, Kathryn Kelly DeWitt, is one of my very dearest friends. She's also an amazingly talented woodworker and designer, with a great eye and even better intuition. She was looking for a simple yet expressive mark to embody all of her various pursuits.

I sketched loosely for a while and then homed in on unique interactions among certain letters. The chosen mark is structural, which references the high-quality furniture she builds, but does not feel overly architectural or rigid. Its interconnectedness speaks to her ability to bridge various disciplines and sensibilities under one umbrella.

In addition to the logo, I created a small icon suite for her website, social media outlets, and other ephemera. They provide a nice contrast to the logo and a nod to the organic elements she uses in her work.

SAINT & SECOND

This project was for a farm-to-table restaurant in Belmont Shore, California. I completed the work while at Helms Workshop. The restaurant focuses on fresh, local ingredients, so the identity embraced a handmade, yet modern, aesthetic.

In the early phases of exploration, I pushed the dynamic between the two words in the name. Noticing that it was rather balanced, I saw an opportunity for a modular logo system, where the type can shift orientation according to application. Horizontally or stacked vertically, the pieces lock up in a solid block that is extremely versatile depending on use.

The iconography is simple and clever, with just the right amount of weirdness to keep things interesting. The oval emblem fits well in various lockups, but it is also strong on its own, adding to the versatility of the design.

For the palette, we chose a nice, earthy terra-cotta red to offset the black and white and enhance the colors of the fresh food the restaurant serves.

KENDRICK KIDD

Kendrick Kidd is a designer illustrator from Florida. He attended the University of North Florida, where he studied graphic design and advertising. After graduation, Kendrick found work at a local newspaper designing classified ads for car dealerships and small businesses. Though he enjoyed the comradery of his coworkers, he found the copious amounts of bursts, loud colors, and bad type unfulfilling. While searching for another path, Kendrick was drawn to the work of advertising agencies in the area. He's since spent the past sixteen years moving pixels and vectors at several ad agencies in Florida, including Shepherd in Jacksonville, where he's been since 2004.

In addition to his ad work, Kendrick spends much of his down time freelancing for himself and Halftone Def Studios (a design boutique in Jacksonville that he cofounded). His most recent work focuses heavily on branding, packaging, and illustrations for craft breweries, action sports companies, and publications.

HOPTINGER

Hoptinger, based in Jacksonville, Florida, is a not-so-serious take on traditional German *biergartens*. The brand works hard to keep things fun, but it still delivers an image of high-quality food and beverage to potential customers. In 2014 Hoptinger decided to launch a poster campaign that coincided with the opening of its Jacksonville Beach restaurant. At the time, no one was aware of the brand or what it stood for. So instead of launching a standard ad campaign explaining its story, Hoptinger took the opportunity to build a legend in the area.

The project started with a list of potential mash-ups between *bier*, sausage, and wartime propaganda posters. *Bier* cannons, keg zeppelins, and hop grenades were just the beginning of what would end up being a mass of absurdly fun imagery that framed the campaign. That, coupled with phrases such as, "No peace in the yeast," and "Spread the wort," set in an arching mono-weight sans serif, tied the serious-but-fun messaging together. When the campaign was completed, Hoptinger wheatpasted the poster series in surrounding areas to generate buzz about its restaurant. After a successful grand opening and positive customer feedback, the owners decided to incorporate the imagery throughout all their north Florida locations.

MODUS

Modus is an Australian company that makes bearings for skateboard wheels. In 2012 it decided to expand its product offerings to include soft goods. Modus was adamant about reflecting the highly functional, hardworking nature of its bearing brand across the new apparel line. It was less interested in trend and more focused on staying true to the company values. After several conversations about direction, a few sketches, and a mood board, a clear path emerged that was heavily rooted in a muscle car esthetic. The parallels between the two rebellious, blue-collar cultures were too strong to ignore. Nearly all the pieces developed since share a bold sturdiness that can be found in factories, machine shops, and backyard garages everywhere. This straightforward, no-BS approach to graphics has helped Modus maintain its earnest hardware brand and successfully transition into the wearables market.

LACHLAN BULLOCK

Born in Tasmania, Lachlan studied visual communication in Hobart and graduated in 2008 from the University of Tasmania. He then moved to Stockholm and has been working in the creative arts industry. Lachlan has strived not only to learn a new language but also to understand the Nordic visual culture.

Today he sees himself as a creative somebody who develops a platform through the use of design, creative thinking, and strategy. Currently specializing in conceptual design with a focus in packaging and identity, he has had the pleasure of developing a vast number of large, iconic Swedish brands and products. This journey has led him to believe that a balance of craftsmanship and creative thinking is the only way to build something that is beautiful while still being thoughtful and engaging.

NOSH AND CHOW

New to Stockholm since 2013, the townhouse restaurant/bar Nosh and Chow offers a variety of gastronomic experiences under one roof. Simply put, Nosh and Chow brings the world to Stockholm.

With no brief and only a week to make deadline, Stureplansgruppen provided two 3-D images of what was to become Nosh and Chow's interior. From this, Nosh and Chow's identity became a sensory exploration of what was to be.

The excitement of contrasts, where the old and rustic blends with a highly modern expression, was the common thread throughout the creative process. The identity combines classic and modern nautical typography with graphic elements closely connected to the characteristics of Stockholm, a city surrounded by water. Nosh and Chow reflects the contrasts of the world: We are all big and small, black and white.

TOWN HOUSE

NOSH AND CHOW

STOCKHOLM

DET ÄR SKIMMER I MOLNEN OCH GLITTER I SJÖN · DET ÄR LJUS ÖVER STRÄNDER OCH NÄS

OCH OMKRING STÅR DEN HÄRLIGA SKOGEN GRÖN · BAKOM ÄNGARNAS GUNGANDE GRÄS

GRÖNSTEDTS LE NATIONAL

Every year in June, Grönstedts releases Le National—its flagship cognac celebrating the Swedish national holiday.

Our objective was not only to design a premium product but develop analog production techniques to deliver a truly special experience that would appeal to all five senses.

The result is a bespoke box with a single locally minted brass coin. Both box and bottle are individually labeled and numbered by hand. To lift the concept further, a celebratory action is embedded in the destruction of the outer box label—by pulling the tarred hemp string and ripping the label, the consumer is forced to destroy something beautiful in order to experience the product inside. In doing this, a new tradition of celebration is born.

Packaging is seen and used every day. It affects our decisions, and it is no small feat to create work that stands out on increasingly crowded shelves. The use of interesting print techniques or the use of materials in an original way contributes to the design as a whole. The heart and soul of packaging is to consider all elements— size, shape, color, materials, design, and so on—while reflecting the brand and product. Here I've selected products that have interesting quirks or details that give them that extra flare and character.

CATEGORY 2
PACKAGING

YANI & GUILLE	46
DEVICE	50
ARITHMETIC	52
JAMIE CLARKE TYPE	54
KELLY THOMPSON	56
PETER GREGSON STUDIO	58
SAM LEE	60
BRANDWAGON	62
CHAD MICHAEL STUDIO	64
THE SHALLOW TREE	68
TOM LANE	70
REYNOLDS AND REYNER	72
SNASK	74
SPASM	76
VAULT49	78

YANI & GUILLE

Yanina Arabena and Guillermo Vizzari (Yani & Guille) are graphic designers born and raised in Buenos Aires. They were both professors at the University of Buenos Aires teaching typography when they began a personal project combining design, illustration, and calligraphy. This led to their collaboration on projects related to lettering and typography for clients around the globe.

In 2012 they graduated from the postgraduate course on typography design at Faculty of Architecture, Design, and Urbanism, University of Buenos Aires. There "Esmeralda Pro" and "Abelina Pro" were born, two typographic projects whose tutors were Alejandro Paul and Ana Sanfelippo and that are currently part of the Sudtipos catalog.

CHANDON

We created lettering design for the packaging lineup of Chandon Argentina, 2015/2016 edition. From the beginning, Chandon Argentina wanted to incorporate a significant twist as part of the complete redesign of its whole packaging line.

For the lettering, separate words were drawn and calligraphied at first. Soon, though, we realized we needed to treat each composition as a whole.

All the processes started manually, with words being sketched, drawn, and written with different brushes. In a second stage, each composition was sketched entirely, then completely drawn and inked. Finally, every piece of lettering was vectorized.

COLD DRIP COFFEE

We designed the identity and package design for the new Cold Drip Coffee, made by All Saints Café, a beautiful and cozy specialty coffee shop based in Buenos Aires.

The design process started with rough sketches that defined the personality of the letter forms. The design was based around the search for a classic, clear composition style, aligned with its top-quality artisanal beverage.

LE BLÉ

Le Blé is a deli restaurant with several locations throughout Buenos Aires, offering homemade foods from its French kitchen. We designed a new line of paper bags and packaging, along with a series of illustrations and lettering that complement the experience.

　　All the handmade letterforms were meant to evoke Paris. We made each piece of lettering after extensively studying traditional-style pastry shop signs—both antique and current—throughout France.

DEVICE

Device is a tight-knit group of creators and collaborators in Winston-Salem, North Carolina, that offers clients a range of heart-pounding design and production skills. They are craftspeople who love what they do. They dare to pitch attention-grabbing ideas that may be out of clients' comfort zones—and then prove they can design, build, print, and launch what they pitch. Device never lets fear get in the way of an amazing outcome.

BUCK O'HAIREN'S LEGENDARY SUNSHINE

Buck O'Hairen's Legendary Sunshine is what happens when a night of moonshine kicks on past dawn. This lightly sparkling pick-me-up is the ultimate hair of the dog, and it's classic Americana. Our hand lettering escorts the eye back to the late-1800s. Medicine-show culture gets a written prescription with sepia tints and hand-drawn graphics that hint at big, bold claims.

MIDNIGHT MOON MUSICIAN GIFT BOX

Piedmont Distillers, makers of Midnight Moon Moonshine, sponsored a series of music events throughout the summer and presented a special artist box of moonshine as a gift to the performers on the tour. We designed the screen-printed wooden box to resemble old moonshiner crates. Nestled inside were three individually wrapped jars of Midnight Moon, branded cups, cleverly designed booklets presenting an overview and the history of the brand, cocktail recipes, and an activity book called *The Great Boredom Bust* to help pass long hours of travel during the tour.

ARITHMETIC

Arithmetic Creative is an award-winning branding, packaging, and design company in Vancouver. It is known for its novel, meaningful ideas that build smart and cool brands rich with cultural experiences and ideas that help consumers live a cultured life.

AMOLA SALT

We were tasked with renaming, repositioning, and overhauling the design of Sea to Sky Seasonings's popular salt collection. The existing brand and packaging system devalued the premium quality of the product.

The name *Amola* was created from the word *amoleh*, the old word for pound-size bars of salt. These had been used as currency up until the twentieth century and were so valuable they were known as white gold. We selected Geared Slab as the main typeface because of its industrial characteristics. Its mechanical curvatures tell the story of a time when salt was imported into old shipping towns.

Blurring the line between necessity and luxury, the end result is a type-focused packaging solution that tells the story of tradition and quality that is optimized to go the distance in sales.

THE GREAT WALL TEA COMPANY

The Great Wall Tea Company approached us to enhance its brand and create a set of customizable loose-leaf tea bags and labeling for its high-end matcha tea.

Inspired by vintage travel stamps and overseas freight packaging, we created an oversized stamp that would serve as a "fill-in-the-blank" label for each of the tea shop's many loose-leaf teas. The stamp enables shop staff to provide extra details and tips to consumers, such as steeping time, date of purchase, and origin of the specific tea, while also offering a design that looks beautiful on kitchen counters.

JAMIE CLARKE TYPE

Jamie's specialty is illustrative lettering that aims to bring words to life with imagery and decoration. With a background in web design, Jamie was previously head of design at Microsoft, Europe. He went on to form one of the UK's top digital agencies and worked with a range of well-known media and technology clients. After ten years with his agency, Jamie decided to retrain. He studied type design at Reading University, and letterpress at the St. Bride Foundation in London. He now lives in Sydney.

FICTUS FARM

To ensure my portfolio of lettering contained a variety of styles, I decided to explore a set of letter designs that expressed a clean, contemporary feel. The letters were first sketched very roughly in pencil to explore various concepts and shapes. The inspiration for each of the designs was quite broad: old Victorian woodblocks, medieval manuscripts, Mexican sugar skulls, and photos from a recent trip to Indonesia.

Once I was happy with the overall style of each letter, I redrew them larger and inked in the details. Then I was ready to digitize them. For the letter shapes, I used Glyphs, a program for designing typefaces. The way Glyphs handles vectors is far more intuitive than Adobe Illustrator, however, I always use Illustrator to draw the decorative elements.

TRENTINO APPLE BALSAMIC

Fictus Farm Estate

Perfect for dipping and drizzling on salads

MADE IN AUSTRALIA 250ml

CARAMELISED BLUEBERRY BALSAMIC

Fictus Farm Estate

Perfect for dipping and drizzling on salads

MADE IN AUSTRALIA 250ml

SWEET CHILLI OIL

Fictus Farm Estate

Perfect for dipping and drizzling on pizza

MADE IN AUSTRALIA 250ml

SPICED ONION BALSAMIC

Fictus Farm Estate

Perfect for dipping and drizzling on salads

MADE IN AUSTRALIA 250ml

CARAMELISED RASPERRY BALSAMIC

Fictus Farm Estate

Perfect for dipping and drizzling on salads

MADE IN AUSTRALIA 250ml

KELLY THOMPSON

Kelly Thompson is a Seattle-based award-winning illustrator and graphic designer. She has worked on a wide variety of projects over the years, but her niche lies in the development of brand identities and package design. She is fascinated by the dichotomy of the digital and physical worlds and how they influence each other. She sees a physical relationship with the world that is packed with meaning, connotation, and emotion, so whenever she is stuck on a project, Kelly reminds herself to get away from the screen and get out into the physical world to draw on these meaningful exchanges. She'll sit at Beth's Cafe and watch how they cut the bread, or pop into the Theo kitchen and notice how they use whole basil leaves to create flavor. Kelly loves being a designer because it's so much more than just sitting in front of a screen—at its root, design is simply being curious about the world and sharing a story with others.

BETH'S CAFE

Beth's Cafe in Seattle is a greasy-spoon diner and neighborhood favorite for sixty-plus years with a lot of visual history to pull from and celebrate. My two main inspirations were vintage bread boxes and the retro, greasy café vibe. The whole diner is covered with paper placemats that customers have colored, giving the cafe a very human, local, handmade feel. With all my work, my goal is to lead viewers through all that storytelling so they have that experience themselves, instead of just telling them what they're looking at.

THEO

Every chocolate bar in the Theo limited-edition line is handcrafted, hand-deposited, and hand-wrapped by a small team of chocolatiers. Naturally, I wanted to convey a human pulse in the packaging while still showcasing the unique flavor profiles. Mexican hand-painted signs for the ghost chile bar, deli chalkboard menus for the bagel bar, the palette of espresso crema for the coffee bar, and so on. Sketching to size was important because the bars fit in your palm. So I printed out a sheet of rectangles to work in and then sketched and created letterforms that nestled nicely within the format.

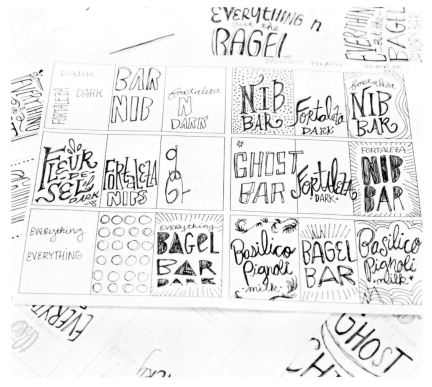

PETER GREGSON STUDIO

Peter Gregson Studio is an independent graphic design studio with a reputation for delivering intelligent, engaging creative solutions. Based in Novi Sad, Serbia, the studio was established in 1999. Today, the studio has eight members working with clients both large and small in Serbia and overseas. The work ranges from packaging design projects for a small local producer to packaging design for wine, children's books, glass, and websites, all the way to corporate identity, brand positioning, retail store design, and branding. The studio's team brings a wealth of knowledge and enthusiasm to every project, and the secret behind the success is honesty and a lot of hard work.

THE MANUAL CO.

We redesigned the existing cardboard packaging for boots, bags, and accessories for The Manual Co., a modern franchise in Serbia that sells handmade, high-quality luxury leather accessories and bags. Because the company produces everything manually, the idea behind the design was to create packaging in the same spirit. Everything on these pieces was drawn by hand.

GiVE LoVE To

THiS C RN®

GOURMET POPCORN
SWEET & SALTY
WiTH a TAD OF BROWN
+ SEA SALT SUGAR
& PURE GOODNESS

2 OZ NET WT. (56g)

ALL natural

FOR MORE INFO
WWW.
INGREDIENTS
DOMATTER.COM

Nutrition Facts

Serving Size (28g)
Servings Per Container: 2

Amount Per Serving

Calories 120   Calories from Fat 45

	% Daily Value*
Total Fat 5g	8%
Saturated Fat 4g	20%
Trans Fat 0g	
Cholesterol 0mg	0%
Sodium 5mg	0%
Total Carbohydrate 20g	7%
Dietary Fiber 2g	8%
Sugars 9g	
Protein 1g	

Vitamin A 0%	•	Vitamin C 2%
Calcium 0%	•	Iron 2%

*Percent Daily Values are based on a 2,000 calorie diet. Your daily value may be higher or lower depending on your calorie needs:

	Calories:	2,000	2,500
Total Fat	less than	65g	80g
Sat Fat	less than	20g	25g
Carbohydrate	less than	300mg	300mg
Sodium	less than	2400mg	2400mg
Total Carbohydrate		300g	375g
Dietary Fiber		25g	30g

Calories per gram
Fat 9 • Carbohydrate 4 • Protein 4

8 57971 00400 7

Made in the USA for:
THE SNACKATERE CORP.
Monroe, NY 10950
www.snackatere.com

WHY THIS C RN?

BECAUSE HEY YOUR LIFE'S CONFUSING ENOUGH.
THAT'S WHY WE'RE NATURALLY **ALL NATURAL** WiTH INGREDIENTS YOU CAN PRONOUNCE AND SPELL TO CREATE AN OUTRAGEOUSLY AWESOME **DiFFERENCE** YOU **CAN TASTE!** QUESTION iSN'T WHY THiS CORN. QUESTION is **WHY ANYTHING ELSE?** NEXT QUESTION is WHAT'S WITH THOSE SHOES? WHO DRESSED YOU THiS MORNING?

WWW.INGREDIENTSDOMATTER.COM
FOR MORE INFO J

CAN'T WAiT TO GET STUCK BETWEEN YOUR TEETH!

INGREDIENTS:

Popcorn, Sunflower Oil,
Evaporated Cane Crystals,
Brown Rice Syrup, Sea Salt,
Vanilla Beans & Honey

NON GMO Project VERIFIED
nongmoproject.org

100% WHOLE GRAIN
24g or more per serving
EAT 48g OR MORE OF WHOLE GRAINS DAILY

CERTIFIED VEGAN
vegan.org

NUT FREE

Certified GF Gluten-Free

U PAREVE

LACTOSE FREE

BE GENTLE to THiS C RN.
WWW.INGREDIENTSDOMATTER.COM

TAKE DOWN THiS C RN
GOURMET POPCORN WiTH CRACKED BLACK PEPPER + LiME & NATURAL KNOW-HOW
NET WT. 2 OZ (56g)
ALL NATURAL

GiVE iN TO THiS C RN
GOURMET POPCORN WiTH TOFFEED CHERRIES & REAL HANDIWORK
NET WT. 2 OZ (56g)
ALL NATURAL

BLAME iT ON THiS C RN
GOURMET POPCORN WiTH ROASTED SWEET RED PEPPERS + JALAPEÑO & AN INSPIRED SENSE OF TASTE
NET WT. 2 OZ (56g)
ALL NATURAL

APOLOGIZE TO THiS C RN JJ.
WWW.INGREDIENTSDOMATTER.COM

GiVE LOVE TO THiS C RN JJ.
WWW.INGREDIENTSDOMATTER.COM

THIS CORN

The task for this project was naming, brand ID, and packaging design for gourmet kettle popcorn. The main goal was to create a witty identity to go with the clever, memorable name that communicates more than the ingredients and taste.

The design elements create a distinct look within the whole category—character illustration instead of appealing photos, a colorful palette, and handwritten copy. Our result was a unique and memorable brand ID and lovely packaging that strongly stands out from the other snack products on the shelves.

SAM LEE

Sam Lee is a Sydney-based hand-lettering artist, illustrator, and designer who visually communicates great ideas. He spends his free time working on lettering projects and shares his process in hopes of inspiring others.

Sam's approach straddles that fine line between art and design, which is to capture the attention of the viewer and leave a memorable experience through beauty and details while remaining thoughtful and relevant in communicating the brand's message. With experience in packaging, apparel, and brand development, Sam uses a handcrafted aesthetic that visually connects people to brands.

RED RADIO BEER

Young Henry's, a brewery based in Australia, crafted a limited-edition hoppy ale named Red Radio using local Australian ingredients to celebrate FBi Radio, a station dedicated to the music of Sydney.

Some decisions were made in a purely strategic sense, such as making the label black and white to cut production costs because all profits were being donated to the radio station. The color we did use was the brand color of the radio station and was intended to bring out the name of the beer. The label's design was fitting to both the brewery's brand as well as the younger crowd being targeted.

Something visually appealing raises interest and curiosity among the crowd, and this design achieved increased awareness for the Sydney radio station.

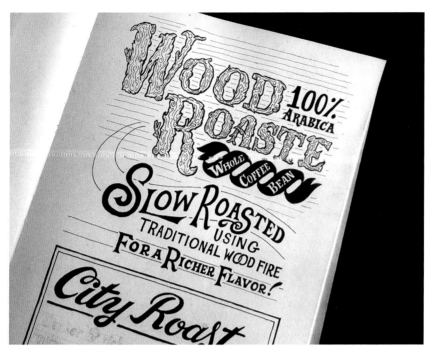

WOOD ROASTE COFFEE

As the name suggests, Wood Roaste is a brand that roasts its coffee beans using wood fire—a time-honored method. The main benefit of slow roasting is that it does not dry out the beans, preserving much of their flavor.

Packaging was designed for Wood Roaste's whole-bean coffee using hand-lettered typography and illustrations to reflect the rustic, organic nature of the product. The sleeves use colors appropriate to the type of roast, and they open up to a poster that informs the consumer of the advantages of roasting coffee with wood.

The traditional wood-fire method requires precision and skill so as not to burn the beans. Based on this, I illustrated the packaging on a single sheet of paper and, aside from changing its color, made as few digital edits as possible to reflect this insight. Whatever little quirks or unrefined edges appeared as a result were left to keep the design original.

BRANDWAGON

Laura Feavearyear, owner of the Auckland-based Brandwagon, is internationally recognized for her work with packaging and brand design. She works during the day for a large media company looking after nine radio brands while running a small boutique agency. This is no small feat—especially because Laura has been visually impaired since birth. Her eye condition prevents her from driving, playing sports, or seeing a lot of what other people see. However, it does not affect her passion, talent, or creative spirit.

DR. FEELGOOD

Dr. Feelgood ice pops are a summer-selfie-ready mix of nutritious and delicious ingredients guaranteed to impress your trainer *and* your snobby food-critic friend. We wanted to make sure the packaging was sustainable, fun, and reminiscent of the good ol' days of traveling medicine men. Each pack from the two products has its own personality, with two different colors, but all have similar elements to make up one family.

The first range of ice pops was codesigned with Laura Feavearyear, Todd Yonge, and Melanie Bridge; the second range design came straight from Laura at Brandwagon. Both ranges presented various challenges, such as making the Body Block product attractive to many different targeted groups, and keeping the ice pop packaging construction simple and sustainable. Each challenge was met in record time and the ranges were out in market with huge amounts of positive feedback and many "mmmmmm yums!"

CHAD MICHAEL STUDIO

Launched in 2014, Chad Michael Studio is a niche design company well versed in the matters of unique branding, package design, and product innovation. The Dallas-based studio is built on the belief that the designer should be equally as passionate about the project as the client.

ST. LAURENT GIN

St. Laurent is a handcrafted spirit whose essence is equal parts mystery and discovery. A Canadian gin with a label primarily in French, the design pulls inspiration from author Jules Verne, along with visual cues from antique encyclopedias, to perpetuate the distillery's depth of knowledge regarding its recipe and distillation methods—as well as its marvelous provenance. A few of the French phrases on the label include "Brave the Unknown," "Abyssal Odyssey," and "Drink the Unlikely."

OLD STANDARD

Old Standard moonshine has the world's first moonshine design printed on fabric. Each label is hand printed, stitched, and numbered for the local folk of Colorado. Old Standard's design is inspired by Prohibition, before whiskey was industrialized and when making it was a craft truly done by hand in the backwoods—a product "for close friends and combustible engines."

PROMINEO

With a limited production of 300 bottles, Promineo whiskey was created as a promotional piece for Chad Michael Studio to send to clients and agencies. *Promineo* is the Latin for "to stand out," and the aim was to develop a label that did just that. The design took many weeks to develop and an equal amount of time to print. The label was printed using letterpress methods that consist of two engraving inks and two foils on Neenah Epic Black stock.

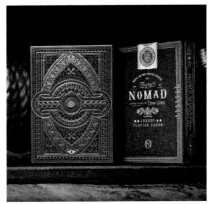

NOMAD

NoMad playing cards were inspired by actual architectural elements of the NoMad Hotel in New York City. From the fireplace in the lower level to the hotel's signature phrase, "Made Nice." The back design, when rotated laterally, forms the shape of an eye—a gentle nod to the Latin phrase at the top and bottom of each card: "Beauty is in the eye of the beholder." Even the interior of the box has a pattern branded with the NoMad logo. No detail was left untouched. Designed by Chad Michael, the deck features a custom vintage design, reimagined jokers, a gold-embossed tuck case, and a stamp bearing the seal of the State of New York. Authentic distressed faces and realistic textures make the cards look like they've been passed down from generation to generation.

THE SHALLOW TREE

Peter-John de Villiers is an artist living in the Norwegian countryside. The Shallow Tree studio rests midway up a mountain overlooking a valley with a fjord in view from the drawing desk. It may be heaven.

Peter-John's iconic style has become an integrated part of Norwegian and international cultures. He has worked extensively with package design, musicians, lifestyle brands, the extreme sports industry, editorial, and advertising. A few notable clients include Carlos Santana, Coca-Cola, Nike, Sony Records, Volkswagen, *Snowboarder* magazine, and YES. snowboards.

GRANS

I collaborated with the FRANK. agency in Oslo to create this iconic packaging for the Norwegian brewery Grans. The concept evoked the traditional hand drawing and lettering of an earlier era for the relaunch of Grans's Christmas beer. The entire label, including the type, was drawn as one piece. The design was awarded gold for packaging in Merket for God Design, a highly prestigious award in the Norwegian design industry.

TOM LANE

Tom Lane, otherwise known as Ginger Monkey, is an independent graphic designer, lettering artist, and illustrator with eleven years of experience. He has worked for an eclectic range of clients—from global commercial corporations to design studios and advertising agencies to small start-ups and individuals. He works closely with clients to produce high-quality crafted artwork, packaging designs, and branding. Tom currently lives and works in Liverpool, UK.

ANTLERS PLAYING CARDS

Daniel and David Buck are American sleight-of-hand pioneers, and have their own store where they sell playing cards and other magic-related goods. I worked with them to develop a new brand of playing cards, Antler. For this deck, we set out to embody the beauty of the great outdoors and were inspired by the wild forests, rolling hills, and snow-capped mountains of northern California.

DARKNESS! WHISKY

I was tasked with creating a label design for the team at Master of Malt, a large online retailer of spirits. Darkness! is one of their own creations, a whisky finished in sherry casks to give it a lighter, sweeter taste. The design needed to allow for variations in the age, type of whisky, and sherry cask used for finishing. I tackled it by creating a master design and supplying the team at Master of Malt with custom type for the different variations or blends and a set of numbers for the age designations. This gave them all the adaptability they needed.

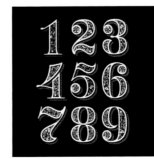

REYNOLDS AND REYNER

Reynolds and Reyner's approach to branding is rooted in the power of design. It believes great design creates a higher-quality brand experience, building meaningful connections between a business and its customers. Reynolds and Reyner delivers innovative design solutions that not only help brands stand out, but also tell clients' stories in visually compelling ways.

Reynolds and Reyner collaborates with its clients to understand their individual needs and elevate the value of their brands through thoughtfully designed experiences. Since forming in 2005, it has remained at the forefront of technology, implementing tailored solutions with effective outcomes. It has offices in Kiev, Brooklyn, New York, and Shanghai.

WALDO TROMMLER PAINTS

Waldo Trommler Paints is a small Finnish company planning to enter the US market. Unlike the majority of existing brands in its category, Waldo Trommler didn't have an established history and believed the key to accessing the market was unique package design. The phrase, "We must stand out!" became the basis for our work on its new brand identity.

Ultimately, we created a brand with no corporate colors. Waldo Trommler Paints simply features common design elements that are recolored in a wide array of bright hues, depending on the application. This helps Waldo Trommler Paints not only achieve its goal of standing out, but it also helps cast the brand as the friendliest paint company on shelves today.

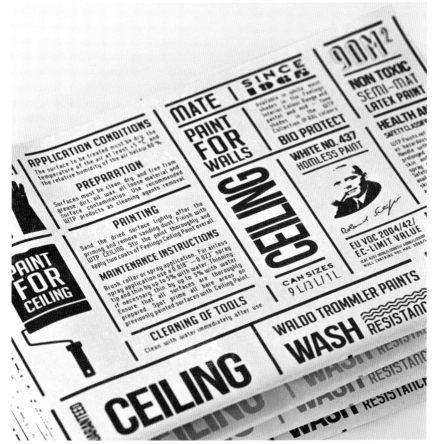

SNASK

The new world order is called Snask. The Stockholm-based Snask strives to challenge the industry by doing things differently. It worships unconventional ideas, charming smiles, and real emotions, and views the old, conservative world as extremely tedious and its biggest enemy.

PANGPANG

At the age of twenty-three, oddball Fredrik Tunedal tattooed PangPang across his knuckles to celebrate the founding of his PangPang Brewery—now Sweden's number one microbrewery. Passionate about hand-brewed beers, Tunedal launched a summer beer series in 2014.

We built the concept for the series around an exotic tiki theme and named the beers appropriately. Our aim is to help PangPang outdo—and outbrew—its competitors through the use of smart branding and gorgeous design. Our client-agency journey has just begun, so stick around—this story isn't over yet!

OUMPH!

Oumph! is part of the new generation of innovative food products taking over the world. It's made entirely from beans. It's insanely good for the environment, easy to cook, and—last but not least—it tastes delicious.

We were brought in by sustainability agency Futerra to develop the identity for Oumph! The brand feels punk and raw because Oumph! is anything but your run-of-the-mill, boring, ecofriendly veggie product. The brand is a revolution and a punch in the face. The graphic identity was crafted and inspired by the look and feel of food trucks and chalkboard scribbles. Oumph! is booming on Facebook. People are raving about the product. Meat lovers are on the verge of turning vegan. Oumph! will change the world, and we are here to help it reach its goals.

SPASM

Spasm is an independent studio that stands for innovative ideas that are strategic and fresh. It thinks holistically, using design and contemporary media as tools for communication with successful results. Spasm studio is a bridge connecting the left and right brain, making creativity both analytical and functional.

Art director Natasha Alimova is a Russian–Argentinean graphic designer living in Auckland, with more than ten years of experience. Throughout her career, Natasha has specialized in brand strategy, brand positioning, fast-moving consumer goods packaging, point of sale, and everything in between that can involve a small or big brand process—always enjoying the process of creation.

ALDERSON'S SAUCE

A fusion of flavor and culture mixed into a tiny, powerful bottle, Alderson's is a boutique hot sauce company with a focus on making delicious, uniquely flavored and memorable condiments. Their products are 100 percent New Zealand-made and handcrafted, using the freshest local ingredients and produce. Our challenge was to create a memorable but simple packaging that will be instantly recognized. Design inspiration came from Central American Mayan art—each hand-drawn illustration was crafted into a chile shape. The use of bright colors helps represent the three strong and differing flavors, while the use of different fonts represents each product's unique personality.

MOREPORK BBQ SAUCE

Often heard in the forest at dusk and into the night, the morepork (New Zealand's only surviving native owl) is known for its haunting, melancholy call to seek a mate. Like the morepork, no cut of barbecued meat should be left unaccompanied—day or night.

No, this isn't a fairy tale or spooky story; this is Alderson's (boutique hot sauce company) Morepork BBQ Sauce. We designed the newest addition to its line of New Zealand-crafted condiments that use only the freshest local ingredients and produce. Building the product concept on a mysterious tale instantly creates a bond with customers and a connection that draws them to the product.

VAULT49

The people at Vault49 create branding, advertising, design, and art for clients, themselves, and the love of good work. Vault49 crafts brands, typography, illustrations, photography, and even the tables the staff work from. Vault49's team collaborates to build strong ideas and stay focused until it has brought these ideas to life—sometimes with their hands, often digitally, and always with passion, honesty, and good looks. The New York–based Vault49 features a diverse group of creative people who enjoy making beautiful, effective work. It's in their bones, it's what excites them, and they're good at it because they enjoy it.

KEG

Sixpoint Brewery is famous throughout the five boroughs of New York City and is fast becoming one the city's most-loved products throughout the United States. The brand heritage is all about craft, thinking differently, and making a big impact with a small budget.

Our limited-edition keg design was created to do exactly that. Sixpoint gained recognition by providing its beer direct to bars only, and what better way to grab the attention of your customers than with a keg design that truly stands out from row upon row of metal cylinders?

GRIND

Diageo approached Vault49 with an award-winning liquor, originally released in 2002, that it wanted to relaunch under the Grind brand name. Our brief was to reposition and redesign Grind to make it more relevant to consumers today. A key challenge was to retain the existing bottle shape and closure or use preexisting stock bottle shapes.

To establish the look and feel, we found shared visual cues between bars and coffee shops. Vintage coffee shop window signs and bar mirrors informed the wordmark and brand icon, while chalkboard art and sign painting informed the bold typographic and illustrative styling on the package front and back.

To retain an authentic crafted feel, we created the label art on a grand scale using a chalkboard. Tiny "flaws," such as uneven strokes, character blemishes, and chalky texture helped retain the integrity of the design process.

Finally, we worked closely with Diageo's technical packaging team to bring the details to life in the print process with a soft-touch label base and expertly executed embossing and metallic varnishes.

Environmental graphics is quite a niche market, but once you are exposed to it, you soon realize it offers a wealth of materials, applications, and possibilities. Being able to work within physical restraints, such as a building, will inspire the most creative and individual work. Considerations for how the building is used by employees, clients, or customers will also influence the design. One of the most satisfying parts of this subject is the final stages, being able to see a full-scale mural or a building-wide signage system take life and become part of the architecture.

CATEGORY 3
ENVIRONMENTAL

GEMMA O'BRIEN	82
ASHLEY WILLERTON	86
BRYAN PATRICK TODD	88
SHED DESIGN	90
BÜRO UEBELE VISUELLE KOMMUNIKATION	92
ADAM VICAREL	94
BEN JOHNSTON	96
ANDREAS M HANSEN	100
CRAIG BLACK	102
JEREMIAH BRITTON	104
JOEL BIRCH	106
LILLY LOU	108
DIRTY BANDITS	110
NO ENTRY DESIGN	112
GED PALMER	114

GEMMA
O'BRIEN

Gemma O'Brien is an Australian artist who specializes in lettering, illustration, and typography. After completing a bachelor of design at the College of Fine Arts in Sydney, Gemma worked as an art director at Animal Logic, Fuel VFX, and Toby and Pete before deciding to fly solo as a commercial illustrator in 2012. Her typographic work takes on a variety of forms, from calligraphic brushwork, illustration, and digital type to large-scale hand-painted murals. A Sydney resident, her advertising commissions, gallery shows, speaking engagements, and global hand-lettering workshops make up her busy schedule.

LAGUNA BEACH INSTALLATION

This hand-painted typographic installation was created for the California's Laguna College of Art and Design gallery in 2016. The show was made up of four key pieces of text drawn from password forms, wi-fi connection error messages, and captcha tests: "Remember Me," "Re-establishing Lost Connection," "Prove You're Human," and five iterations of "OK." Viewers were invited to engage in a physical reading experience by walking through the space, decoding the phrases, and finding links among them. Conceptually, I liked the idea that this digital language can be so mundane yet, when taken out of context, speaks to bigger questions of lived experiences—relationships, human connection in the digital age, the desire for legacy and meaning. The original drawings for the show were made using a combination of techniques, including calligraphic brush lettering, illustration, and manipulation of digital fonts, which were then scanned and projected onto the gallery walls and painted over a week's time.

VOLCOM ART LOFT MURAL

In 2014 I was invited to paint a mural in the
art loft of the Volcom Stone headquarters
in Costa Mesa, California. The brief was to
capture the energy and creativity of the
artists who work in the space. The process
for creating this piece started with rough
layouts in Adobe Photoshop and a small
sketch on paper. I then camped out in
the space overnight to project the image
and hand-painted the final piece in
twenty-four hours.

ASHLEY WILLERTON

Ashley is a Newcastle-upon-Tyne, UK–based multidisciplined designer and craftsman with a focus on hand lettering, traditional sign writing, and reverse glass gilding. With a passion for design history and a particular interest in the sign writing and gilding artistry of the Victorian era, Ashley has built a reputation for his traditional approach that, wherever possible, employs the same methods and materials used more than a century ago. He believes this aspect of his work is fundamental to keeping the standards and integrity of the craft at the highest possible level.

LOLA JEANS

In 2015 I was approached by Newcastle Creative Agency Unit44 to design and hand paint an old-fashioned, heritage-style sign for clients Lola Jeans Food and Cocktails. The brief was to use the staircase wall to display signage for the establishment's new Prohibition-style bar that would be opening in the forthcoming months. As with all my projects, after I've thoroughly digested the brief, I begin drawing rough sketches to get a sense of composition, letter interaction, and style.

As the style of the new bar was themed around the Prohibition era, I knew I wanted the lettering style to reflect the kind of branding, signage, and typography that would have been commonplace in 1920s America. Having researched this design period in the past, I'd learned that America's hand letterers, at the time, were heavily influenced by design of the Victorian era, particularly when it came to their use of ornamental detail and elegantly constructed script lettering. To give the sign extra punch and majesty in low light, I used 24-karat gold leaf for the filigree that forms the T's crossbar and LJ monogram.

1901

I worked closely with the new owners of 1901 to help reinvent their cafe's image as a high-end bistro. Uniquely located inside an unused section of a church in Newcastle-upon-Tyne, UK, it has incredible space and natural light, and the huge sandstones walls previously had ugly steel signage affixed to them. Knowing the brand and the company ethos well, I knew immediately what kind of route I wanted to explore.

Since the church that the bistro sits in was established in 1901 (hence the name) and I would be painting directly on the original walls, I wanted to pay tribute to this design era so the sign looked like it belonged on the wall rather than sit uncomfortably on it. Working with a limited color palette, as was common in those days, I chose to bring the sign to life with elaborate Victorian elements, such as the ornamental border and scroll that intertwined with the lettering, to create an interesting and unique structure. This theme was strengthened with elegant, well-balanced lettering that I embellished with subtle drop shadows and highlights for extra visual appeal.

BRYAN PATRICK TODD

Bryan Patrick Todd is a freelance American designer from Kentucky. He specializes in lettering, illustration, and environmental design. He is a self-taught designer whose early days in design were spent in a small sign shop, combined with long nights and weekends devoted to learning and studying his craft. As his freelance career began taking off, Todd conceptualized his first mural in collaboration with sign painter Kirby Stafford. The mural was installed on the side of a three-story building in a progressive area of Louisville, Kentucky, in 2011. The pair have partnered together on murals ever since.

HIGHLANDS

This was my first commissioned mural, in the Highlands neighborhood of Louisville, Kentucky. The mural is approximately 60 ft (18 m) wide and 40 ft (12 m) tall. The idea was to make a statement about the neighborhood, in one of the city's most vibrant areas, full of shops, boutiques, and restaurants. The building was already painted black and I wanted to create a design that complemented the building but also stood out in a bold way. To bring the design to life, I enlisted veteran sign painter Kirby Stafford. The end result has turned the corner into somewhat of a local landmark, playing a recognizable role in the city's identity.

SMIRNOFF

This mural was designed and installed for Smirnoff's Global Art Project initiative. The idea was to create a piece that was inclusive, allowing people in Tokyo to be a part of the installation. In light of the approaching spring season in Japan, I loved the idea of people from the community submitting their hopes and wishes for the coming year and including them in the artwork.

I traveled with Kirby Stafford to install the mural in the busy, energetic area of Shibuya in Tokyo. As soon as we arrived, it was as if everything came together perfectly. The weather, people, and location made for an easy installation. Even more, having the chance to interact with the community and share my work in such a beautiful city was an incredible opportunity. The final piece measured 38 ft (11.5 m) wide and 18 ft (5.5 m) tall, and took three days to complete.

SHED
DESIGN

Shed Design is made up of interior designers and architects who've been designing and delivering environments for some of the world's leading companies since 2000. They are straight-talking, smart-thinking creatives who work across residential and commercial markets, specializing in branded interior design. Above all, they focus on originality and innovation in everything they do. Shed Design is passionate about the creative process and loves to make things happen. It has offices in London and Shanghai.

EASTER EGGERS

CREAM LEGBAR

RUMPLESS GAME

YAMATO GUNKEI

nankin shamo

PLYMOUTH ROCK

WISHBONE

Grade II-listed Brixton Market is now thriving with food outlets, each featuring its own cuisine, and doing it particularly well. Wishbone creates fried chicken, part of the soul of Brixton, and delivers it with care and style. With Wishbone, we set out to reinvent fried chicken and the place in which you eat it. The whole concept was, "Take a simple thing, and make something beautiful." Inspired by the vibrant indoor market feel of Brixton Market, colorful elements of graffiti are set against an honest material palette of oak and galvanized steel. Warm rough-sawn oak timber lines the walls, like an updated version of traditional wood paneling, circling an exposed concrete floor.

BÜRO UEBELE VISUELLE KOMMUNIKATION

Founded in 1996 by Andreas Uebele, büro uebele visuelle kommunikation is an agency based in Stuttgart, Germany, that is active in all areas of visual communications, with the focus on visual identity, signage and wayfinding systems, corporate communications, and exhibitions. In recent years, the agency's work has been honored with more than 300 national and international awards. In 2003 büro uebele won the Red Dot: Grand Prix award for communication design, one of Europe's foremost design prizes.

ADIDAS GYM

Smarter, brighter, and better—those are the walls of the new Adidas gym. Colorful decorations made of numbers and letters get the rooms in the company's gym into shape, boosting energy, pulse, and power. Up to 33 ft (10 m) tall, the graphic elements we designed are more than just feel-good wallpaper, but, instead, they actively communicate with the gym's users as they warm up or chill out. The colors are taken from the world of sport, but all jumbled up. In some rooms, bright ideas can be found in the shape of huge illuminated numbers on the ceiling—54 ... wasn't that the year of Germany's miraculous World Cup win? Whatever—there's plenty here to think and talk about.

ADAM VICAREL

Adam Vicarel is a designer and artist based in Denver, who specializes in the creation of hand-drawn, illustrative typography. Vicarel has been featured in numerous international publications and on websites for his lettering and custom typographic works. With a thorough background in fine arts, he likes to tread the line where art and design collide. Vicarel, who is constantly on the go, draws inspiration from his international travels and the mountainous outdoors, with which he regularly surrounds himself. A true lover of making things—whether for personal use or a client's work—he is a designer who is constantly creating.

BE FEARLESS MURAL

The *Be Fearless* mural was commissioned by Spin, a creative agency based in Denver. It wanted a mural painted on its largest interior wall that spoke to the agency's fun atmosphere and its clean, innovative design aesthetic. I put the mural together in Adobe Illustrator, where I was able to move elements around and tweak their scale, placement, and colors until I landed on a design we thought best represented the agency. Once the design was finalized, I used a projector to trace the typographic portion of the mural onto Spin's 19 ft x 8 ft (5.8 x 2.4 m) wall. I completed the mural in two four-and-a-half-hour days. This was the first mural I had ever created, and I learned a lot about the process of creating a small sketch for a large-scale piece, as well as the importance of considering the environment for which the piece is created.

BELIEVELAND

The *Believeland* mural was a self-initiated chalk mural drawn on the exterior façade of a brewery in my hometown of Cleveland. As an important American manufacturing center in the early-twentieth century, Cleveland began to decline in the 1970s as companies moved away. The city today is experiencing a resurgence, as millennials move back to the city with a drive to start small businesses, breweries, and other entrepreneurial endeavors. The influx of businesses into the region has led to growing economic prosperity in Cleveland, and the city has recently adopted the word "Believeland"—a hybrid word stemming from "believe in Cleveland."

I began this piece by refining a small sketch on paper, and, ultimately, decided to use a grid system to redraw the wordmark on the chalkboard wall. First drawing a baseline, X-height, and angled lines for reference, I began drawing the word "Believeland" with a very gestural chalk sketch. Then, I went back over the piece numerous times, slowly drawing, erasing, redrawing, erasing, and refining the letterforms. Once the skeleton of the wordmark was created. I added the orange drop shadow, and then, finally, went back through my design to erase any remaining imperfections.

BEN JOHNSTON

Canadian-born Ben Johnston is a 29-year-old self-taught designer who grew up in Cape Town, South Africa. After a brief stint in industrial design, Ben started focusing on traditional graphic design with a preference for creating typographic illustrations from scratch. His industrial design experience gives him the ability to break the confines of 2-D and 3-D, enabling him to bring his designs to life. With more than seven years' experience in the creative industry, Ben's portfolio includes a prolific selection of completed projects for renowned ad agencies and major overseas clients. Ben is currently based in Toronto as a full-time freelancer.

LULULEMON MURAL

This piece was created for Lululemon in Vancouver and was used for its annual conference where employees gather to celebrate their successes and build team morale. I was lucky enough to have a team of their designers and artists assist me in painting the piece. The whole piece had to be done in two days.

Because everyone's skills differed when it came to using a paintbrush, I decided to use large ink markers instead. This allowed everyone to create crisp edges and for the piece to look seamless. The sketch was done the night before and then we painted for two solid days until it was finished. It was a great brand piece to work on and a great change to have a team to work with to create the piece.

PAN AM GAMES MURAL

The main idea for this mural was to create a phrase for the 2015 Pan Am Games in Toronto that would translate into French and Spanish and also inspire the athletes while training during the games. We came up with "Prepare for Greatness," which perfectly sums up what the athletes are doing during their training.

The wall is 140 ft (42.6 m) long, so each translation had to be painted as large as possible to cover the area. After running through various concepts and styles, I chose to move forward with a casual brush lettering done in the gym brand colors of the YMCA. I managed to do the entire piece over five days, from sketch to completion, as we were under a very tight timeline. The sizing and sketch of the wall were very time-consuming as there was no room for error. From there I used rollers, large brushes, and indoor house paint to complete the piece.

ANDREAS M HANSEN

Andreas M Hansen is an incorrigible creative who specializes in web design, art direction, calligraphy, and crafting brand identity. Used to working primarily in a digital medium, Andreas first pursued calligraphy for its physicality, drawn in by the tactility of ink and paper. After noticing a lack of usable and fun tools for designers to learn the many typefaces, he designed and created his own app, Font Nerd, which gamifies the process. With a diverse list of clients including theQ Camera, *Elle Denmark*, Friday Smart Lock, and Beo Play, he is always looking for new opportunities. Currently based in Copenhagen, he has lived and worked around the world, most recently in Hong Kong.

WHATEVER YOU ARE BE A GOOD ONE

I was approached by Founder's House, a start-up industry coworking in space based in Copenhagen, with a blank slate mural project. I chose the quote, "Whatever you are be a good one," by Abraham Lincoln as the content because I think it speaks to everyone. Regardless of who you are or what your job is, you are chasing perfection or, at least, success. This quote sums up the energy and vitality of the space and the people who work in it. Once I decided on the quote, I employed my usual process while creating the mural. I hand lettered it in pencil and with a brush on paper before even thinking about putting it on a wall. After this, I sketched a grid onto the wall. Working from my sketch, I sketched the letters onto the wall with pencil, and then hand drew them with various brushes using black paint.

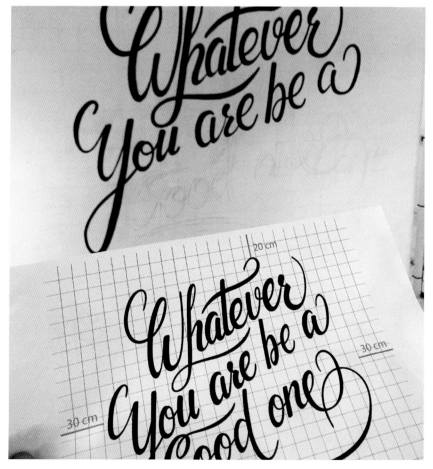

CRAIG BLACK

Craig Black is a Scottish-born graphic designer, illustrator, and typographer. Having spent the first few years of his career in leading design agencies gaining experience in print to motion and everything in between, Craig currently runs his own design studio in London. Known for his bespoke and innovative typographic illustrations, visual identities, packaging, installations, and murals, Craig's versatility has provided him the opportunity to work on a varied mix of projects with local and international clients of all business backgrounds.

SLICKS BARBERSHOP

Slicks BarberShop wanted a unique approach to using social media to compete in the difficult beauty industry. The aim was to enhance the company's business by creating an enticing design that would intrigue customers. So I created a unique typographic and lettering design for the barbershop's front window, technically crafted by hand to resemble a vintage barbershop style with a modern twist.

I utilized two typographic layouts that appear on two of the largest glass window panels that are tied together by a geometric frame. I hand-sketched the design to full scale in pencil followed by pen on paper using a grid format to ensure correct positioning and scale. To complete the design on glass, I placed the design on the outer window and reverse painted the concept outline in acrylic paint pens. Once the outline was complete, the sketched design was removed from the outer window, which revealed the design more clearly for highlighting and the intricate detail work.

CHASE BARBERSHOP

The Chase Barbershop contacted me to create a double-sided chalkboard design for the opening of their brand new barbershop in Essex, London. The brief was to create a handwritten illustrative typographic design that would act as the main feature of the shop's signage display. With the barbershop's industrial feel, using multiple colors would have been lost within the brand, so I was inspired to push a black-and-white monochrome feel to create more depth within the design.

The process started by sketching out the initial concept of how it would visualize on the board and then applying this concept to the board. I hand sketched the design to full scale in pencil using a grid format to ensure correct positioning and scale. As the client's vision was to have a handwritten chalkboard design as exterior signage, consideration had to be made to the weather. As a result, I decided to use acrylic paint pens to keep a vibrancy to the design, followed by a coat of varnish to protect it.

JEREMIAH BRITTON

Jeremiah Britton was born in Portland, Oregon, and raised in the heart of the rustbelt in southern Michigan. He has developed a blue-collar work ethic that is reflected in his craft and passion for making. Currently, he lives in Brooklyn, New York, and is the director of art and graphics at WeWork, where he leads a team of artists and designers who create environmental art and graphic installations for WeWork's offices all over the world.

APPBOY MURAL

Appboy is a mobile-marketing and app optimization platform with a new headquarters in midtown Manhattan. The designers at Homepolish allowed me to work directly with the Appboy design team to use some of their existing iconography and slogans to develop a custom typographic mural for their kitchen and lounge space. I created more than forty custom pieces, did original copywriting, and illustrated a few of the icons, in addition to using lots of great phrases and icons provided by the Appboy designer Ahmed Gamal and team.

HUSTLE LONDON

WeWork is always using bold and inspiring phrases to keep the members of its coworking spaces motivated. This piece was originally inspired by traditional sign-painter lettering and was meant to be one large and simple sans serif piece. However, a day before installation, I learned that the wall I would be painting was covered in box molding as a major design feature of the space.

So just twenty-four hours before installation, I reworked the piece to change type styles each time it met the existing molding on the wall—kind of a great testament to the WeWork "startup-y" culture of making changes on the fly, having multiple styles, and conforming to preexisting situations. The epitome of "hustle."

JOEL
BIRCH

Joel Birch is a multidisciplinary artist hailing from Noosa in Queensland, Australia's Sunshine Coast. He grew up in a small town before moving to the coast, with a deep love of and interest in old signage and typography. He also fell in love with graffiti the first time he laid eyes on it. After numerous years lurking in the shadows with a backpack full of spray paint, he began crossing over into graphic design, at first self-taught, before applying his love of letters to more illustrative work. He still loves the deconstruction and reconstruction of letters that graffiti provides today, but oftentimes you will find him painting large-scale, typography-based murals, such as the ones on this page, or honing his brush skills trying to embrace the spirit of the sign painters of old.

SHINE ON

This was a "love" piece for me. I'm lucky to have a few outside spaces to paint around my house, including my local skate park where this was painted. I'm in a band called the Amity Affliction, and so it was easy for me to come up with words. These are taken straight from one of our songs. It's a nice sentiment and perfect fit with the area and the space. Like every other mural or painting I've done, it was completely unplanned. I don't sketch them out. I don't do anything aside from picking a color palette, and sometimes I don't even do that. Instead, I just throw my paint in the car, head to wherever I'm painting, and see what happens. I like the organic way the paintings evolve in that regard. Sometimes, however, this apporach sees me fail completely. I can only laugh when that happens—thankfully, it happens less and less as I get older and paint more.

LILLY LOU

Lilly Lou is a London-based street artist and designer with a passion for letterforms, bright colors, and positive vibes. She developed a distinct script-lettering style while studying graphic design and illustration at Nottingham Trent University. After graduating in 2011, she took on a full-time graphic design job at We are Why (then KentLyons) and, in her spare time, experimented with a spray can to develop her style in a different medium and scale. It wasn't long before she began making her mark on the streets of London, trying to put a smile on the faces of the general public with relatable words and sayings. After two years in the industry, Lilly went freelance and has since been producing a variety of mural and experimental design projects.

SAVE THE ARCHES

#savethearches was a huge campaign that saw many artists use their talents and styles to help generate awareness and protest against Network Rail's massive and unaffordable 300 percent rent increases in Brixton. "Stop the Evictions" was my contribution to this campaign. I tend not to work up a sketch too much before painting, as I enjoy working it all up on the wall, developing the shape of the letters into the given space as I go along. I spend a good amount of time getting the lettering right before proceeding with the fill; it's important to get the sketch on the wall right at this stage, as mistakes in the flow, sizing, or kerning only get worse if not corrected early on. For this piece, I blended three pinky-purples together through the letters, followed by a white outline to make the lettering pop, and then I finished the piece with a cast shadow to lift the lettering off the background. I love using my work to make a difference to communities. It's rewarding to achieve such positive results with our art collectively.

DIRTY BANDITS

Annica Lydenberg of Dirty Bandits is a San Francisco–based designer, illustrator, and sign painter who is deeply obsessed with type. From Brooklyn, New York, Annica moved to San Francisco to study sign painting. As a graphic designer, she had paid close attention to typography for many years, but now focuses on using a wide variety of mediums for mark making. Phrases that Annica paints are inspired by traditional show card writing, her love of puns and word play, and 1990s hip-hop. She works with painting, chalk, screen printing, and pen and ink, pulling stylistic influence from an ever-growing photographic library of found type composed largely of vintage and contemporary signage.

FREEMAN MURAL

This chalk mural for the FreemanXP office was based on its mission statement. I pulled individual words and phrases that held their own and then created a large grid of frames to hold each unique word or phrase. The wall was unified by the frames and consistent coloring and shading throughout, but each frame had its own permanent style and layout.

Parts of the mural were done with poster paint markers and parts with chalk. This gave the wall a large range of tone, despite it all being white, allowing the words to pop and protecting the overall integrity of the wall from bumps and smudges as people move through the hallway. There was a fire alarm and an outlet in the wall that I chose to incorporate as well, just for fun, rather than pretend they weren't there.

ZETTA MURAL

The Zetta mural stairwell was executed as part of a mural competition. There were seven artists who each painted one floor of the stairwell. We had only forty-eight hours to complete our floor and our theme was San Francisco. This stairwell had many different textured surfaces so I had to use a combination of brushes for the smaller text and tight borders, and spray for the larger fills and gold color. Text was placed based not only on available surfaces but also in consideration of how a visitor would move through the space.

NO ENTRY DESIGN

No Entry Design was created as an alias for the design work of Mr. Never Satisfied, a street artist based in Brooklyn, New York, who travels excessively. Nev (nickname), tired of barely getting by while living off his personal art, decided to learn a new craft that he could keep separate from his personal work. Because his portfolio showed such a range of different disciplines and he was working under the alias of a company name, he ended up having lots of people approach him, thinking No Entry was an agency. Instead of avoiding projects that were too big for one person to handle, Nev reached out and hired friends to help.

TRANSFORMER WALL

In the winter of 2014, I decided to get out of the New York cold and took a trip to New Zealand and Australia. To my surprise, my friend Annica of Dirty Bandits happened to be visiting Melbourne during the same time so naturally we decided to paint together. I couldn't possibly have felt more welcomed during my stay. My buddy Dean Sunshine connected me with his friend Laki who owns a popular vegetarian restaurant in Fitzroy called the Vegie Bar. Laki was in the process of converting an old transformer factory into another restaurant/bar. Because Dean hyped me up so much, Laki decided to hire us to restore the old signage up top and go to town on the façade beneath. This was more of a "for fun" project than a commission.

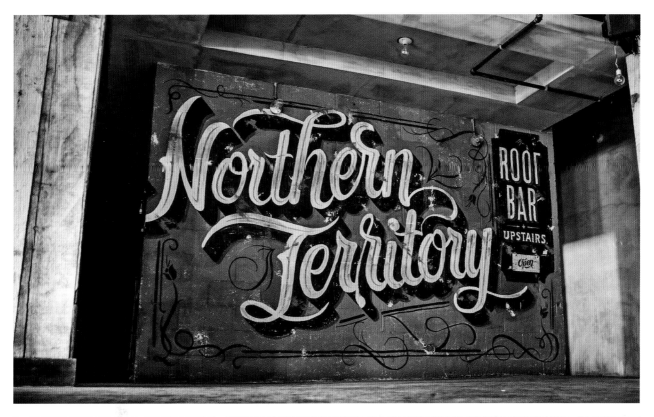

NORTHERN TERRITORY

Northern Territory was a full-on branding project that started when I was approached by an Australian named Jamie who was opening this bar, along with a guy named Jon, who owned another popular bar in Williamsburg, New York. Jamie is also a bit of a street artist, and when I got to know him, we discovered we had a lot of friends in common. We became good friends during the project and have since worked together on others. Although I was commissioned to do everything for Northern Territory—logo, menus, signage, website, and photography— I always find that the painting tends to be the most fun.

GED PALMER

Ged Palmer is a lettering artist and sign painter based in London. His life-long fascination with letterforms has seen his work evolve, shifting through the disciplines of lettering , typography, calligraphy, and sign painting, with the aim of discovering how letterforms were traditionally made. Having established a career in custom logotypes and lettering for book covers and advertising, Ged began working with a brush in 2012 and has since traveled to various countries to learn sign painting and gold leaf gilding techniques.

Today his practice focuses primarily on hand-lettered designs and sign painting for restaurants and independent businesses where a custom-made identity can be anything from a logo to gold-leaf windows. Ged's work has been recognized by the International Society of Typographic Designers, the Type Directors Club, and various publications worldwide.

ARTISTS & FLEAS

This project came about through my New York friends Travis W. Simon and Caetano Calomino. I was passing through town and Travis had this 90 ft (27.4 m) mural project. So we sat up one night and drew the lettering between us. We agreed on the style pretty quickly and, when we worked up the artwork, you could not tell who had drawn each letter— which doesn't happen every day! The artwork was projected using an overhead projector and painted by Caetano, Will Van Zee, and Rich Soffar, as well Travis and me. Using a transparent glaze with tinting medium for the cast shade was what really made this design pop off the wall. Good times!

THE WEIRD & WONDERFUL

The Weird & Wonderful is a "rarities and taxidermy shop" based near Manchester, UK. The owner commissioned an ornate gilded door panel for the shop and wanted me to capture some of that florid, detailed work made in the UK during the late 1800s. It was a challenging piece to make—100 percent hand painted with mirrored and matt gilding, patterning in the gold (12-, 18-, and 24-karat), and, finally, some inlays of pearl. Let's just say driving it there was a hair-raising experience!

The act of creation for creation's sake is not only therapeutic but also essential for self-development. Self-initiated projects are extremely important for practicing designers. Some artists and designers are lucky enough to be commissioned and given free rein to create what they are known, loved, or respected for—which is a privileged position to be in. But to break free from clients and briefs is important so you can explore your own ideas, some of which may not have seen the light of day yet. It could be purely to test your skills with new software or to widen your horizons with new skills.

CATEGORY 4
SELF-INITITATED

LAUREN HOM	118
CHRIS PIASCIK	122
CARL FREDRIK ANGELL, A.K.A. FRISSO	124
JAMES LEWIS	126
WASTE STUDIO	128
MARTINA FLOR	130
ROB DRAPER	132
DARREN BOOTH	136
BOHIE PALECEK	138
IAN BARNARD	140
JUSTIN POULTER	142
SARA MARSHALL	144
BOBBY HAIQALSYAH	146
LUKE LUCAS	148
VELVET SPECTRUM	150

LAUREN HOM

Hom Sweet Hom is the studio of Lauren Hom, a California-born, Brooklyn, New York–based designer and letterer. Known for her bright color palettes and playful letterforms, Lauren has created work for clients such as Google, Starbucks, AT&T, YouTube and *Time* magazine. Her work has been recognized by Communication Arts, the Art Directors Club, the Type Directors Club, the One Club, and the Webby Awards. Lauren also authors the popular blog (and now book) *Daily Dishonesty*.

Lauren finds she's happiest when creating; so, when she's not working, you can find her baking yummy things, selling your ex-boyfriend's tears, or lettering for lunch around New York City. Lauren's motto is, and will always be, "Work hard, snack often."

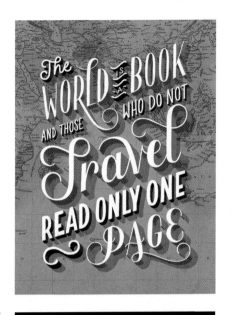

6 LETTERS, 26,000 MILES

Early in 2015, I decided I wanted to travel more and started planning a year-long trip around the world. As you can probably guess, it wasn't going to be cheap. Though I planned to work the entire year, I knew having extra money would be helpful, but traditional fund-raising seemed so boring and needy. So, I came up with an idea to fund-raise for my travels that combined my interests and skill set.

I created and sold a series of hand-lettered posters with my favorite quotes about traveling. I named the project 26 Letters, 26,000 Miles because of the length of the alphabet and the circumference of the Earth. I launched it six months before my trip and ended up raising enough money to pay for my airfare for the entire year.

You can't **DISCOVER** *New Oceans* unless you have the **COURAGE** *to Lose Sight* of the **SHORE**

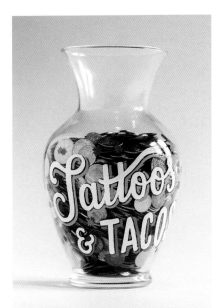

WIGGY BANKS

The idea for Wiggy Banks came from the coin jars my roommates and I always kept in the living room for spare change. A lot of people have them but never really have an intended purpose for the money. Usually we'd use it for bus fare or the laundromat. Boring, right? I counted all the coins in our jar one night and realized we had more than $100, which was actually enough money to buy cool stuff. I immediately thought of all the useful things I could buy, such as books and art supplies, but quickly realized I'd probably just end up buying wine and cookies like any other twenty-four-year-old would. I wrote down a list of some other funny and true things that my friends and I spend our money on, bought some jars and 1-Shot paint, and Wiggy Banks was born.

HOW IT WORKS

1 YOU PUT YOUR DAILY SPECIALS ON A SIGN LIKE THIS!

2 I'LL COME BY & *Letter* YOU A PRETTY SIGN WITH YOUR SPECIALS FOR THE DAY

SOMETHIN' *Yummy* HERE!

3 IN EXCHANGE FOR A TASTE of THOSE SPECIALS! IF I WRITE "BEST LASAGNA IN NYC," YOU CAN PAY ME with A PLATE OF LASAGNA.

WHY?

YOU NEED A *Tasty* LOOKING SIGN. I LIKE TO DRAW. I LIKE TO EAT. I NEED A *Tasty* TASTING SNACK.

Send an email to me at:
LETTERFORLUNCH@GMAIL.COM
PLEASE INCLUDE YOUR NAME, THE NAME + ADDRESS OF THE EATERY, AND THE DATE YOU WANT YOUR SIGN LETTERED! *MUST BE BOOKED AT LEAST 3 DAYS IN ADVANCE

WILLLETTERFORLUNCH.COM

WILL LETTER FOR LUNCH

One Sunday afternoon while walking down a busy avenue in Brooklyn, New York, on the way to brunch with a friend, I noticed almost every restaurant had a chalkboard sign out front with their brunch feature and drink specials for the day. To be frank, most of them looked like a hungover hostess had written them with her nondominant hand. A magical little lightbulb appeared. Restaurants give away free food all the time. I'm a letterer. I've never done chalk work before, but if I can do it on paper, how hard could it be in chalk?

And with that, the Will Letter for Lunch project was born. The concept was simple: I'd go around to New York City eateries and offer to re-do their chalkboard signs in exchange for the exact menu items I lettered. So, if I lettered a sign that said, "All-You-Can-Eat Sushi," I'd get paid with all-you-can-eat sushi (which is a lot, by the way). If I lettered an entire cocktail menu, then it was going to be an interesting day.

I printed fliers and walked around for weeks pitching myself to restaurant managers around Brooklyn. The word leaked through the design and restaurant communities and over the next year, I practiced my chalk lettering and ate delicious free food at more than thirty New York City eateries. I gained so much from the experience: restaurant industry connections, improved chalk skills, and, of course, weight.

CHRIS PIASCIK

After starting his career as a graphic designer at award-winning studios in New England, Chris accidentally became an illustrator. He's pretty happy about that. This strange transformation was a result of his daily drawing project that he started in late 2007. In fact, the Sturbridge, Massachusetts, resident still posts a new drawing every weekday. Chris ran successful Kickstarter campaigns that allowed him to self-publish two collections of his daily drawings, *1,000 Days of Drawing* (2012) and *Another 1,000 Days of Drawing* (2016). In addition to those drawings, he draws for clients including Coca-Cola, Nike, Ogilvy, and Nickelodeon.

Chris received his MFA in illustration and BFA in graphic design from the University of Hartford's Hartford Art School, where he is currently an adjunct professor. He is art directed by his three rescue dogs, Duke, Biggie, and Bluie.

Sitting down and drawing everyday changed my life. I'm not being glib—it's true. Nine years ago, when I sat down to do my first daily drawing, I didn't know it was my first daily drawing. I was working as a graphic designer in Boston and living in a tiny apartment with a cat, some bikes, and gigantic rats. Okay, the rats were outside—*but* I could see them from my window.

I had a sketchbook, and I drew a picture on the first page. I took a bad photograph of it and put it on my website. The next night, I did the same thing. Then I decided to draw every night (okay fine, not every night—every Monday through Friday). Now, nine years later, as a result of this self-initiated project, I work for myself, and there are no more rats. The one constant is that I've continued to do the drawings and, as a result, they've become my main source of promotion.

For the past couple years, I've been working almost completely digitally with a Wacom Cintiq, drawing directly in Adobe Photoshop. Though I consider myself a digital artist, I use these tools in a very analog way. I sketch with a brush that looks and feels like a pencil, and I draw over my sketches with a brush that mimics the same felt tip markers I used to work with. I say this because I want to make it clear that, although I work digitally, it's simply for efficiency.

When I begin a lettering composition, I write out the word or phrase quickly just to get an idea of where it can break and how the words relate to one another. Sometimes I'll create a shape or framework for the lettering to fit within. Writing the word quickly and loosely in the shape helps me create a template for my illustrative lettering. Sometimes this is easy. Sometimes I create fifty sketches trying to get it right.

CARL
FREDRIK
ANGELL,
A.K.A. FRISSO

Carl Fredrik Angell, a.k.a. Frisso, is a graphic
designer from Rykkinn, Norway, with an MA
in visual communication from Design School
Kolding, Denmark. His specialties are hand
lettering, type design, and sign painting. In
2013 he went to Boston for a three-month
apprenticeship with Josh Luke and Meredith
Kasabian of Best Dressed Signs to learn the
craft of sign painting. Taking what he has
learned, Carl Fredrik is making his mark on
the surrounding visual landscape by bringing
hand-painted signage back to the city. He
is very stylistic and designs new, creative
typography wherever letters are needed.
Everything he creates is handmade and shows
great skill and knowledge of typography.

LAID BACK LOUNGE AND ROLY POLY

I often find self-initiated projects to be the most satisfying. As I am my own client, I have the freedom to do whatever I like and experiment more with different styles of letters and layouts. If I'm working on a quote for a typographic composition, I start by splitting the sentence up into different parts. I then visualize where each part of the sentence will go in a roughly sketched layout to make sure it feels natural to read through the design. I never have a set plan from start to finish.

I make changes throughout the process, and, to me, that's what keeps the process interesting and fun. You are making decisions constantly, which forces you to be sure you have made the right one before you paint or draw out the design with a pen or marker. You can't just press Ctrl-Z (undo) and start again. This is a great way to build confidence in your decision-making skills, which can shorten the process when working with clients.

JAMES LEWIS

Comfortably juggling a graphic design degree in Cardiff, while freelancing alongside his studies has provided James Lewis with the opportunity to explore many different elements of the visual arts, but none have captivated him quite the same as typography. Without any prior knowledge or skill in art and design, his initial interest with type grew out of a dislike of his own handwriting. James set out to improve it by learning cursive, but the beauty of copperplate calligraphy sidetracked him. He was inspired to trace the beautiful letterforms, and soon after he was hooked on drawing typography. (His handwriting, however, remains only semilegible.) James has taught himself how to digitize the typography he draws into vectors, which helps define the crisp, minimalistic style he has adopted in recent hand-lettering artwork and prints.

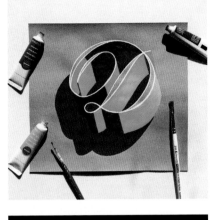

LETTERS

My love for crafting a single letter as a unique piece of artwork emerged when I was learning calligraphy. I would write the same letter over and over, either with a brush or a pointed copperplate nib, until I got the desired effect I was looking for. I knew back then that the key to producing the best letter was always getting the smallest details right. As time went on and my style developed, I spent more time drawing typography rather than writing calligraphy.

I was becoming more inspired by the three-dimensional work of sign painters and their ability to make every letter a piece of art in its own right. One day I decided to draw typography on craft paper with paint markers and was instantly attracted to the contrast and depth I could create by combining black and white within the confines of a single letter. I explored shading and depth in detail, which helped me cast realistic shadows to the letters, allowing them really stand out on the page. I plan to continue pushing the boundaries of what I can create within the constraints of a single letter. The restrictive nature of the challenge pushes me continually to incorporate wider influences, which I appreciate a lot as a creative person.

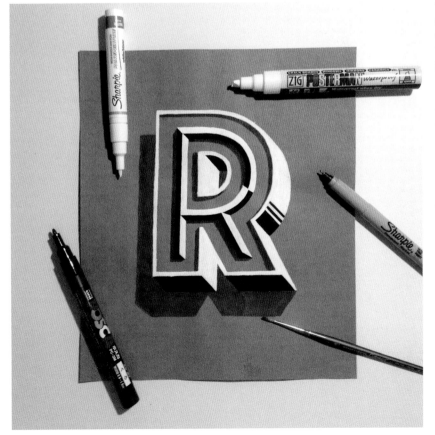

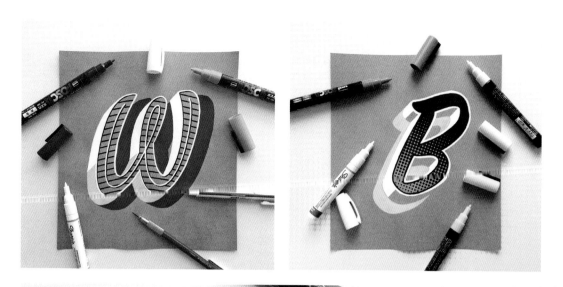

WASTE STUDIO

Waste Studio, based in Nottingham, UK, was founded in 2006 when former print designer and illustrator Norman Hayes decided it was time for a small, energetic, creative agency built around ideas.

The ambition was to create an agency that provided its clients with vibrant design, fresh, creative thinking, and a culture that showed care and consideration for clients and team members alike, while maintaining balance between a timely turnaround and creative excellence.

RECONSTRUCTED LETTERFORMS

A modular typeface is an alphabet constructed out of multiple sections called modules. This project focuses on the architecture of typographic design. The process of deconstructing letterforms to a series of simple modular segments allows the reconstruction of more interesting form; through rotation and overprinting a wide range of exotic letterforms is created, some more legible than others.

Having spent the majority of my career making custom typefaces, I wanted to investigate further how the letterform can be broken down into a series of simple parts. "Reconstructed Letterforms" is a self-initiated project defined by playing with conventions to find new creations. The desired outcome illustrates the breaking down and building up of a letterform, allowing people who are not type designers to understand how letters are constructed.

This special project combines traditional silk-screen printing and typography. Using this method to reconstruct the parts allowed us to engage the audience in the "reconstruction" process.

The brief to our audience was simple: Tell us your favorite letter, and we'll design and print it live in front of you.

All of the module parts were exposed onto one fixed silk screen, meaning the only way of lining up the parts was physically to move around the medium on which we were printing, in this case, a t-shirt. The lining up was done by hand, creating a level of uncertainty which, in turn, led to some beautiful mishaps and misalignments.

MARTINA FLOR

Martina Flor combines her talents as a designer and illustrator in the drawing of letters. Based in Berlin, she runs a leading lettering and custom typography studio. She is also the founder of Letter Collections and cofounder of the project Lettering versus Calligraphy.

With a master's degree in type design from the Royal Academy of Arts in the Netherlands, she dedicates much of her time to teaching lettering and type design internationally. She is the author of *Lust auf Lettering*, published in 2016 by Verlag Hermann Schmidt (to be published in English as *The Golden Secrets of Lettering* by Princeton Architectural Press), and presents her work at conferences and holds workshops to help designers grow their skills.

MAKE IT HAPPEN

At the end of every year, I work on a salutation for clients and colleagues—some interesting piece of work that I want to make sure they will keep because it is just too great to throw away.

In this instance, I wanted to experiment with laser cut. I had seen the machine at a workshop and was fascinated by how precise it can be as a printing technique.

The main challenge was to create a decorative design that would hold together through the multiple cut-outs. The designs usually created for stencil are normally very bold and chunky. I wanted to walk away from that and design an ornamental artwork with lovely detail, yet make the job as a stencil.

Paper selection was also essential for the final look of the design. A 350 gsm recycled cardboard satisfied the job of staying rigid despite the multiple incisions.

The message "make it happen" is reinforced by the call to action of the cardboard stencil. Each card was used to spray the accompanying envelope with gold paint. I spent about two days in my studio spraying cards and it was worth every minute.

ROB DRAPER

Rob Draper is an artist and designer based in the UK who specializes in hand lettering. He has launched a range of reusable ceramic coffee cups and sells prints and originals through selected galleries. Rob has been a guest speaker on professional practice in art and design and delivered sessions on design and creativity to a wide range of audiences—from graphic design students to prisoners. He is passionate about creativity and lettering.

COFFEE TIME

It's a long, old story, but this whole project started intentionally as a funny mix of personal development and self-promotion. After a long career in brands and agencies, I was finally going it alone, and, after years hiding under the umbrella of a brand name or agency, was fairly anonymous. Initially I had a website, and while it had work on it, it wasn't completely the work I wanted to embark on. Yet every available moment throughout my life I was always drawing, stockpiling sketches—mainly letterforms.

Starting a business on your own can be quite an isolating process, and I was filling in the "no client" gaps with my standard go-to activity: drawing. I started publishing some work online using Instagram in the hope it would creatively push me further toward where I wanted to be and also to act as a virtual shop window. First with "Coffee Time," and then with "Create More," I developed two personal projects that I revisit and enjoy to this day, based on the challenge of finding things that shouldn't really be drawn on, or things with little or no value, and then spending as long as possible embellishing them with lettering.

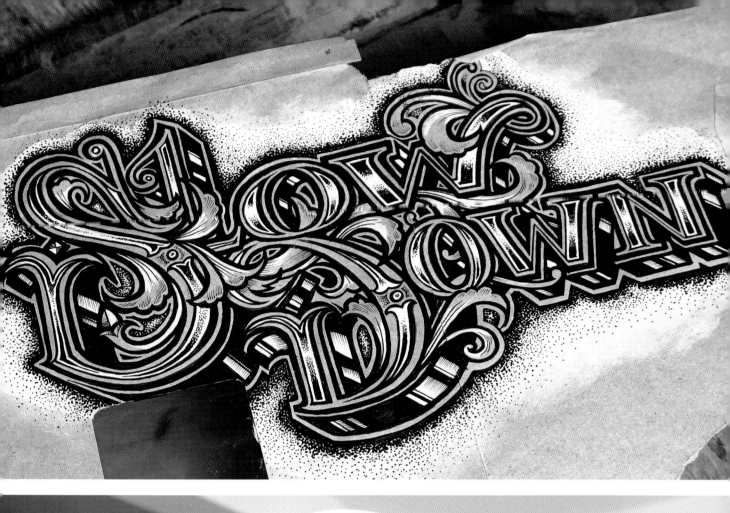

DARREN BOOTH

Darren Booth is a Canada-based illustrator and lettering artist. His handcrafted, expressive—yet controlled and succinct—style has enabled him to collaborate with clients such as Google, Coca-Cola, AOL, Target, McDonald's, and Disney. He's also provided his distinctive work for high-profile clients Steve Martin and Willie Nelson.

LETTERS

For these self-initiated projects, I wanted to create pieces that were bold and iconic. My work always begins with thumbnails to help sort out ideas and compositions. From there, I develop the sketch further to a tight line drawing that I can transfer to printmaking paper where I render the final artwork with acrylic paint and found collage. For these pieces, I also wanted them to be legible and feel solid, which is all sorted out during the sketch stage, sometimes editing the sketches in Adobe Photoshop. For the most part, I have only a rough idea for the color palettes and I don't get a true sense of the overall palette, mood, and tones until I've blocked in all the areas with color. Once the piece has been blocked in, I start to glue down and build up the collage elements. Each collage piece is meticulously cut and considered one at a time for size, placement, color, pattern, and shape. The collage elements serve multiple purposes, such as creating texture, controlling how the viewer's eye moves around the composition, as well as helping evolve the color palette.

BOHIE PALECEK

With a life-long artistic streak, Australian Bohie Palecek began her professional career as a graphic designer. In 2011 she moved away from computers to pursue a hands-on approach, and she now focuses on traditionally crafted design. She works in a variety of mediums using traditional sign painting techniques to produce work ranging from branding and illustration to large-scale murals.

Bohie is inspired by the aged and faded façade of Australian heritage, the recklessly fun-oriented skate park culture that breathes "Ride Fast/Get Loose," and an appreciatively slow-paced lifestyle focused on living light of foot. Always looking to learn and develop her practice, Palecek travels interstate and overseas seasonally to collaborate with her clientele, while maintaining her studio base in Adelaide, Australia.

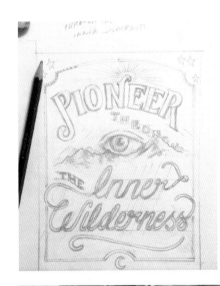

PERSONAL WORKS

Working full time as a creative, I'm not able to maintain self-directed projects consistently, choosing instead to schedule in an art exhibition while taking time off work to focus completely on art making.

With a new concept in mind, I reread my personal journals, dissecting the stream of consciousness into what's relevant and what's necessary. Sometimes it's only a few words or a quick sketch that captures the energy I want to explore. I'm always refining ideas into their basic form before sketching the final pieces.

The next step is finding harmony in the relationship between concept, content, and intention. I explore different mediums, lettering, and colors to find the combination that represents the concept intuitively (as opposed to literally). I want the piece to communicate the message without relying too heavily on the words. This stage involves research through museums, art galleries, driving back roads, or looking at old signage.

Once established, the execution of the artwork is more about headspace. The concept behind an artwork might be a hard-earned lesson, but I still want the vibe of the piece to be positive and approachable. Being connected and stoked with my surroundings and having energizing conversations is a must for me to allow the creativity to flow. Before hitting the studio, I might head out for some solo camp vibes or have a session with new friends at the skate park . . . whatever I can do to remind myself not to take it all too seriously and just have fun.

IAN
BARNARD

Ian Barnard is a calligrapher and hand letterer living in Crowborough, UK, working for such clients as Speedo, Hellmann's Mayonnaise, and Adobe. Constantly pushing the boundaries of what can be achieved with pen and ink, Ian experiments with anything and everything he can get his hands on to use as an instrument to letter with or on.

He loves teaching, entertaining, and empowering people to improve their lettering skills through short videos on Instagram and YouTube. Ian drinks way too much coffee and has a library of typography books that would make any designer jealous.

CALLIGRAPHY PROJECT

At the beginning of 2016, I wanted to see whether I had the skills to apply my calligraphy to a range of different surfaces using a variety of paint markers, brushes, and pens. I started to collect random objects I found in charity shops, jumble sales, or on the internet to letter on.

I would initially lay out the design on paper, usually a quote or a few words associated with the object. Once I was happy with the design, I would prep the object, whether that was roughing up the surfaces so the paint would stick or spraying it a contrasting color so the type would show up.

I recorded my progress through time-lapse films to post on my social networks. This meant I had only one shot to do it right, as I didn't have the time to go through the process of respraying that object.

Most of the time it would go well, but there was one incident where the paint marker leaked over a black backpack leaving a nice gold blob, which I then had to incorporate into the design. This taught me how important preparation is, knowing your tools inside out, and not rushing the process.

Off the back of this self-initiated project I've been commissioned to create similar items for people. It's great knowing I can take an everyday object and turn it into a piece of art just by adding my calligraphy to it.

JUSTIN POULTER

Illustrator Justin Poulter specializes in hand lettering and illustration. Growing up in a village by the sea and completing his studies in Cape Town, South Africa, he landed his first job at an award-winning studio in London. After spending three years there, he moved back to his homeland and headed up a studio in Cape Town. In 2014 he went freelance, where his style of illustration and lettering won him a number of international clients. In what might be the final move, he recently came back to London, where he now works out of his studio in Stoke Newington.

SELF-INITATED WORK

Most of the commercial work I get is illustration focused, sometimes with accompanying type. This is why over the eight years I have been working, I love doing self-initiated typographic work when I have time. Whenever I'm doing self-initiated work, I still try to think of it in a commercial sense, trying to imagine what a client's needs would be. With lettering, the main concern is always legibility and finding the balance between that and style. I love experimenting with this and seeing how far I can distort a letter until its barely legible, yet still reads quickly enough for the viewer to get it immediately. The way I do this is I draw letters while trying to imagine what existing typefaces look like in my head and add a bit of my own flare during the process.

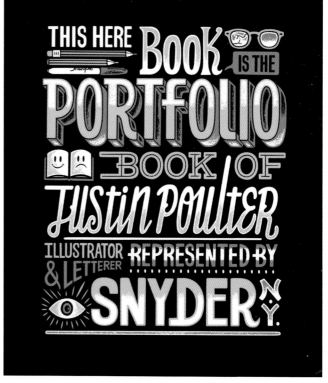

SARA MARSHALL

Sara Marshall is a letterer and calligrapher based in Auckland. She graduated from Auckland University of Technology with a bachelor's degree in graphic design. It was here that she studied under notable calligrapher Peter Gilderdale. She is known for her award-winning lettering project, Brand by Hand, where she reimagined ten famous brand logos by hand. Her favorite tools to experiment with are ruling pens and brushes because, in her words, she is impatient and impulsive. She enjoys the instant gratification of working fast and taking advantage of the happy accident.

CALLIGRAPHY IS SEXY

Calligraphy Is Sexy is a personal project that explores non-traditional calligraphic styles (all ten words are written, not lettered/drawn). Self-initiated projects like this one have been important for my growth as a calligrapher. By setting myself a brief of ten sexual innuendos that describe calligraphy, styled appropriately, I gave my practice some purpose. The project then became one of problem solving and design, which I had to figure out how to execute through calligraphy.

With an end vision in mind, I began cycling through tools and making marks. It is always this hands-on, experimental part of the process that inspires me and gives me ideas to build on. After deciding what a final word will look like, it becomes a test of my ability to create it. This project had me working at all different scales with a range of tools. I had to hone and practice flat brush techniques, which I normally try to avoid (brush manipulation is hard!)—especially Roman majuscules (Slow). I also doubt I would have cut notches into a marker so I could practice some 3½ in (9 cm)-tall Beneventan Lombardic minuscule (Kinky). And even less likely to grab a pair of stockings and revert to finger painting with my pinky (Messy). It was also an opportunity to try the technique of writing with water and letting droplets of ink bleed through it (Wet). These new challenges are in addition to the considerations I would normally take when it comes to calligraphy—consistency and legibility. In projects like this, I find I pay more attention to my technique than I would in my regular practice in a bid to reach that final outcome I'm really satisfied with.

RAW

Rhythmic

kinky

Rough

BOBBY HAIQALSYAH

Bobby Haiqalsyah is a designer, illustrator, and letterer based in Melbourne, Australia. Originally from Indonesia, Bobby combined the vibrant aesthetics of his culture with the design education and history he received in Australia.

Bobby's career began with a lot of self-initiated projects and exploration to learn the tools, the visual vocabulary he loves to work with, and to find the right influences that help create the best results. Through these explorations, Bobby assembled a humble portfolio of illustration and lettering that impressed people more than his design or advertising work. These sentiments encouraged him to approach his current artist representative to take the work to the right people.

This was the start of Bobby's journey creating projects either for himself or for fun, but he aimed for platforms where he could creatively explore as well as reach an audience. It was clear from the beginning that his typographic pieces had more traction than any other styles he explored, so Bobby began seeking project initiatives and competition where he could create additional typographic pieces.

MELBOURNE

I was approached by the fine gentleman behind Betype, a blog dedicated to typography. They started an initiative for which designers around the world made a piece based on their local area. As a resident of Melbourne, Australia, I wanted to typographically represent the capital of the "garden state" and the home of Aussie rules football. I knew the piece needed to be in the shape of an oval because football is played on an oval field.

First attempts felt like the swashes that filled the oval space were too separate from the typography. Once I established a mono line look inspired from copperplate calligraphy, the oval design started to make sense. Although I can't include enough flora to represent the garden state, I felt the birds were enough to suggest the lush garden that they frolic in. This exploration has brought so many inquiries and interest my way and it came from the simple love of the city I've spent more than half my life in.

Type Fight is a platform that was created for two designers to bout with one another, one letter at a time. Fellow designers and members of the general public can vote for their favorite letter rendition. This platform allowed me to create styles that were unique and also exposed me to a broad audience, as my opponents might come from all different parts of the world or industry. Notable work I gained from my appearance on this platform included apparel work for Harley-Davidson.

LUKE LUCAS

Luke Lucas is a Melburnian, now based on the northern beaches of Sydney, with a self-made career spanning two decades. In the late 1990s, he cocreated *Fourinarow Magazine*, an inline skating publication that sold worldwide. With two other partners, he started *Lifelounge*—a combination creative agency, online creative culture portal, and glossy print magazine. It was through *Lifelounge* that he began to experiment with conceptual illustrative typography, custom lettering, and type design, and it wasn't long before he was attracting illustrative type briefs from agencies, publishers, and brands across the globe. Today Luke is an award-winning creative who juggles being a dad to two young boys with surfing and full-time freelance lettering. His regular clients include Nike, Target U.S.A., *Esquire*, the *New York Times*, and the *Washington Post*.

THE IMPORTANCE OF SELF-INITIATED PROJECTS

I would never be able to pay the bills doing the kind of work I love if it weren't for self-initiated projects. While studying for an associate's degree in computer-aided art and design (and as ill-informed as we were about publishing, graphic design, and desktop publishing software), a friend and I decided to start a print magazine. We were forced to learn fast and immersed ourselves in this project for the next three years. In between classes and scattered sleep, we published eight editions, distributed the magazine to fourteen countries, and launched our design careers.

Through this project, I was introduced to lettering, publication design, and the business side of design. If I had not taken that gamble to try something new I would not be where I am today. It's through self-initiated projects that we have the greatest opportunity to grow as creatives, and self-initiated work is as important today to my continued development as it was twenty years ago.

These days most of my commissions and commercial work are inspired by previous work in my folio, and, for the most part, it's rare to find a client willing to allow me to experiment with a new style or technique. This is one reason that self-initiated projects are critical to my growth as a commercial artist. Without offering diversity in your folio, clients will continue to ask you to do variations of the same ideas. I find that to be a one-way ticket to becoming creatively stagnant.

Outside of the opportunity to learn and experiment, self-initiated projects let me create something free from the restrictions often applied to commercial commissions. The work is not trying to sell anything so it doesn't need to fit within a particular format or adhere to specific guidelines. There's no reason for its being other than creative expression—and even if you're not learning something through the process, that motivation for expressing creativity is food for any creative soul.

VELVET SPECTRUM

With some sort of benevolent Willy Wonka-esque energy, Luke Choice's every creation lodges into your perception like an everlasting gobstopper, a storm of golden tickets. One look turns into a hypnotic daze, which turns into a slack-jawed smile, and an affirmative, slow head nod. Like cutting a veil between gritty reality and the cotton candy world we dream about. Though surreal, it's all held together with a confident gravity. Vibrant, yet never loud; cheeky, but never flippant. Fantastical, sans escapism. The New York–based Velvet Spectrum offers you a pair of Technicolor lenses and a chance to see the world beyond its artwork infused with the same playfulness. It calls attention to beauty inherent within its form, and, as an audience, we are transformed. Though the vibrant colors and textures transcend our daily perception, they discerningly refocus our attention back to the infinitely expressive nature of reality.

SCRIBBLES

I find it easier to express myself visually rather than verbally, and these typographic pieces are glimpses into my personality and what inspires me. They can be personal messages to those I care about, music that inspires me, or humorous quotes I jot down. As a series, it has taught me to pay close attention to moments in life that need to be recognized and gives me a way to acknowledge them. My focus is on marrying the words, colors, and energy to convey the intent behind each artwork and what I want the audience to take away from it. I find it so important to have my own voice in my artwork, somewhere I have complete control and allow myself to be vulnerable and communicate on a level I feel comfortable with. This series is more a form of personal expression than a creative exercise.

This section offers students and current designers inspiration and ideas for projects to have fun and grow with. All the briefs take inspiration from the categories in the book; hopefully they will inspire you to tackle one with your own personal style!

Not all of the nitty-gritty information is included, such as the wall dimensions for the environmental brief or the ingredients list for the packaging brief. I want you to take the initiative and create those aspects yourself. At the end of the day, the briefs are meant to inspire you to try something new or build on skills you already have—the outcome is not the main concern.

I hope you can have fun with these lighthearted projects in which the only goal is self-development and the act of creation!

CATEGORY 5

REAL-WORLD BRIEFS

BRANDING BRIEF	154
PACKAGING BRIEF	155
ENVIRONMENTAL BRIEF	156
SELF-INITIATED BRIEF	157

SPONTANEO

SPONEEEEO

Rhythmic

Spontaneous

Spontaneous

SPONTANEO
us.uss

Rhythm

Rhythm

Rhythmic

Rhythm

Rhythmic

Messy

Messy

Kinky

RAW

Calligraphy
is
sexy

Calligraphy
sexy

in kinky

RAW RAW

Raw Raw RAW

RAW

S L

Messy

Wet W W Wet

Wet WETII Wet

WET

Rough

DIRTY

Rough

Rough

Dirty

Wer

W E E I

W W

Wet

BRANDING BRIEF

For this brief, you'll rebrand the well-established business Monterosso Gelateria. Take note of the visual clues and themes to guide you during the project. Take initiative to create content or be experimental with your designs. The brief is meant to give you a starting point and general direction; it's up to you to fulfil its potential. Consider mocking up business cards or other stationery and signage early in the project to help get a feel for where it's going and whether the solution has legs to see it through to the final round.

BRAND NAME

Monterosso Gelateria

BACKGROUND

Monterosso Gelateria is an Italian chain of boutique gelatto shops. Currently it has three stores along the Italian Riviera, in San Remo, Portofino, and Cinque Terre, as well as one in Milan. Long established and initially a family-run business, it wants to rebrand and refresh its current outdated and inconsistent look with something more up-market, classy, and fashionable to better reflect its clientele.

Using long-established traditional Italian techniques to create fresh and flavorful gelato, its products boast twenty exceptional flavors—from the traditional to the more adventurous—for which only the best organic ingredients are used.

THE CREATIVE CHALLENGE

Proud of its heritage, Monterosso wants to project the look of the Italian Riviera across its boutiques. Using the fantastic painted building façades found across the Liguria region as inspiration, Monterosso wants to capture this same feel in its identity and stationery package. This should then flow through the brand's storefronts, menus, and other collateral. So as not to get stuck in the past, this classic style needs to be combined with a contemporary approach, keeping Monterosso Gelateria modern and future proof.

In recent years, the boutiques have attracted more of a jet-set customer, perhaps because of the way the gelattos are displayed—like works of art swirled, dressed, and decorated to the highest standard. Playing on the display's unique selling point, Monterosso would like to take advantage of its popularity by reflecting on the high standard of its gelatto display with an equally high standard of design.

AIMS

Rebrand Monterosso Gelateria

Respect the Riviera region's influences

Combine the tradition with a modern outlook

Instill consistency throughout the design

TARGET AUDIENCE

Customers are affluent, with the occasional celebrity, but the brand also attracts people seeking high-quality gelato, including the high numbers of summer tourists willing to spend a little more on treats.

DELIVERABLES

Identity and stationery package

Menu and flavor labels

Signage

Employee uniforms

ADDITIONAL INFORMATION

Monterosso is interested in suggestions involving store interiors, from refrigerators to furniture, so its brand remains consistent and appealing to its audience. Competitors include Steve's Ice Cream, Salt and Straw, Amarino Gelato, and Chocolat Milano.

PACKAGING BRIEF

This brief asks you to create labels and the carrier for the small craft beer brand Ragnor Brewery. The brief is quite loose, giving you an idea of the brand but not the details. This frees you to decide what bottles to use, to curate and research the content throughout the project, design the look and application for the label(s), and, finally the shape, look, and style of the carrier. Everything here is up to you; so have fun and immerse yourself.

BRAND NAME

Ragnor Brewery

BACKGROUND

Ragnor Brewery is a small Norwegian brewery based in Oslo. Ragnor wants to overhaul its six-bottle packaging. The brewery established itself during the craft beer revival of recent years. Its small runs of limited-edition flavors and types have helped secure it as a favorite among Norwegians and the artisan community. Now looking to spread its wings and appeal farther afield, a selection of its most popular beers will have a packaging design refresh optimized for the European market.

THE CREATIVE CHALLENGE

Ragnor Brewery would like a specially designed series for its IPA, bitter, and lager brews. Your challenge is to design the labels and the custom carrier they'll be sold in. For optional extras, you may want to look at a cap design or specialist finishes, such as glass embossing. The designs will need to work alone but also sit together.

Ragnor Brewery positions itself mid-range with an up-market, yet artisan, feel. The brand is sold in local pubs as well as contemporary bars, and even festival sites. It prides itself on having a more unique and artisan feel, often putting design and artistic flare ahead of practical, legible design. In the past, it has commissioned illustrators and artists to collaborate with designers on its labels and packaging. This time it is after a typographically led series of designs, but is keen to see illustrative elements and embellishments.

AIMS

Establish the brand in Europe

Appeal to the target market

Evoke curiosity

Depart from the traditional beer bottle designs

TARGET AUDIENCE

The typical consumer is predominantly twenty-four- to thirty-five-year-old males bored of the usual beer brands. They are interested in trying and tasting new approaches to beer, and they usually buy from independent retailers as they look to support local artisans.

DELIVERABLES

Three label designs (IPA, bitter, and lager)

Cap design

Carrier artwork

ADDITIONAL INFORMATION

Often, the branding or identity for Ragnor Brewery has been styled to fit with the current label and design; Ragnor seeks a consistent logo but individual bottle designs. The three bottle types are IPA, bitter, and lager. Each can have its own special name that you create or they can simply be named "Ragnor Brewery IPA."

ENVIRONMENTAL BRIEF

This brief asks you to design environmental artwork for a well-established motorcycle company. Things to consider include whether the artwork fits with the company's vision and with the building itself—the two need to exist side by side. Also, put yourself in the employees' shoes. Consider the ways they might use the area and what they would want to see. How people use the building offers real insight into what content you use. Also consider materials and how they can add impressive elements to the artwork.

BRAND NAME

Bristol Motorcycle Company

BACKGROUND

Bristol Motorcycle Company (BMC) is a classic motorcycle company established in England in 1954. BMC has just opened a new headquarters in Brooklyn, New York, to join those already in London and Sydney. BMC, long known as a family business, prides itself on its traditional manufacturing techniques and quality-over-quantity products—products that stand the test of time. The timeless style and charisma of these bikes is what attracts and keeps countless customers across the world.

THE CREATIVE CHALLENGE

Bristol Motorcycle Company's new office in Brooklyn, New York, is a large converted factory. It contains many old features, such as exposed brick and original wood and steel beams. There are newer, more modern attributes, such as an atrium at the reception and a bespoke cafeteria.

The client wants a three-mural theme to run throughout several spaces, bespoke artwork is required for each space. BMC is celebrating its first venture into the American motorcycle market, so it wants the work to inspire all new employees. BMC is proud of its history and wants the murals to maintain a timeless aesthetic that points to both the company's heritage while being inspired by its future.

AIMS

Inspire clients

Create a talking point of the building

Motivate employees

Reflect and respect the geographical area

TARGET AUDIENCE

BMC's main audience is the slightly more mature young professional, who has a higher-than-average disposable income, and who considers himself both fashionable and practical. BMC favors products that are authentic and honest and that have a more of a traditional aesthetic.

DELIVERABLES

Three murals in three building areas:

Reception

Cafeteria

Boardroom

ADDITIONAL INFORMATION

These three murals need to have a linked theme. Although they need to have a similar visual style, the content could be a story, or quotations, or even parts of BMC's manufacturing history. These murals can be all, or predominantly, typographical, and illustration work could be a possible route. Materials are also important to consider—think about how the building and each section will be used by employees and clients. Competitors include Royal Enfield, Ural Motorcycles, Triumph Motorcycles, and Harley-Davidson.

SELF-INITIATED BRIEF

This self-initiated brief is designed to give you a reason to push your limits, stay focused, and develop your practice—whatever it may be. It should encourage you just to have a go at an idea that's been floating around in your head, without consequence or fear of the outcome. After all, nothing ventured, nothing gained.

BACKGROUND

This brief is your brief. Self-initiated projects are important for development and skill progression; they help you explore new ideas with no time limits, deadlines, or external pressure—unless, of course, you add a time limit!

Pushing your creative mindset will enable you to explore areas you have not been before. With only your own demands and desires, "practice makes perfect" has never been more true.

The difficulty with these projects is not only keeping the ball rolling, but also not being too precious about the outcome. Approach the project with the mindset that the work you are creating is part of a journey. The first piece you create might not look or feel like you want it to, but you can't explore new techniques and create high-quality work without first mastering the process. I often say, "process is just as important as product" when referring to your own design practice.

THE CREATIVE CHALLENGE

Essentially, all of the briefs in this book are self-initiated projects, and, although they have clients, the outcomes are still dictated by you. Category 4, the self-initiated chapter, helps you see what other designers have created, the reason behind the projects, and the approach taken.

Using that chapter as inspiration, you can begin to work out what area you might like to develop for yourself. This could be anything from creating a project that makes you try new software or use different materials—anything that places you out of your comfort zone. Designers often try setting deadlines for projects like these, for example, a letter a day or a quote poster each week. The difficulty is maintaining this approach.

AIMS

Develop self-practice

Use new materials

Explore boundaries

Try new techniques

TARGET AUDIENCE

Whoever you want!

DELIVERABLES

Whatever you want!

ADDITIONAL INFORMATION

Set deadlines for yourself. Treat this brief as you would any client brief. Otherwise, it may just be pushed back and put off, so schedule time for it. Don't expect miracles in your first attempts; everyone has to start somewhere.

ACKNOWLEDGMENTS

I'd like to thank everyone involved at Rockport Publishers, from Jonathan and Mary Ann, my editors, to Anne, my creative director, and to Cara, for managing the project.

A special thank-you to my girlfriend, Natalie, who has been extremely patient and has helped me throughout this project. Finally, thanks to you for reading! Having people purchase this book and enjoy its content makes me very happy, indeed.

ABOUT THE AUTHOR

Leaving Nottingham Trent University in 2010 with a first class honours degree in graphic design, Alex Fowkes worked for several agencies before establishing himself via a project that would change his working life—the Sony Music Timeline.

The award-winning British designer was approached by one of the biggest music labels in the business, Sony Music, and commissioned to create a design that would chart the music label's history from 1889 to 2012. He quit his full-time job and spent the next six months planning, developing, designing, and producing his vision for Sony's headquarters. Once completed, the internet did what the internet does best—carried him and the project across countless countries, design blog's, interviews, and various other types of exposure.

Fast-forward four years to this, his second typographic publication. Alex feels fortunate to design for companies such as Urban Outfitters, creating amazing retail spaces across Europe, and advertising campaigns for companies such as Fila in Japan; work with O2 Academies on its music venues across the UK; publish work in many books, magazines, and online media, as well as create limited-edition designs for the likes of Coleman and new brand ArtSac. "To say I've been lucky is an understatement," he says. "Being able to create the work I love to do for interesting clients around the world makes me feel very fortunate, indeed."

ALSO AVAILABLE

Drawing Type
978-1-59253-898-0

The Art of Spray Paint
978-1-63159-146-4

Sharpie Art Workshop
978-1-63159-048-1

Universal Principles of Design
978-1-59253-587-3

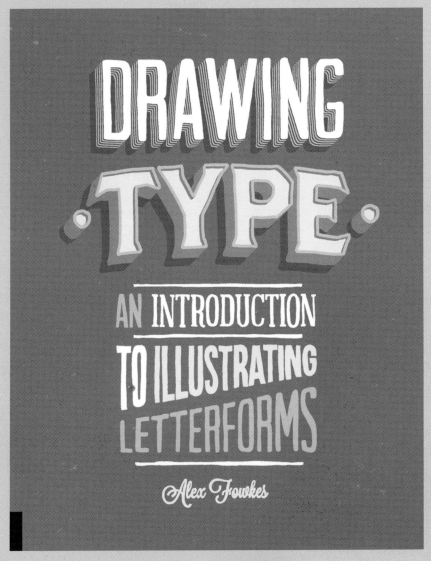

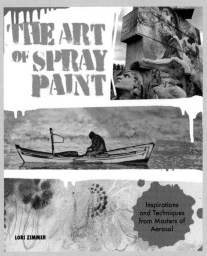

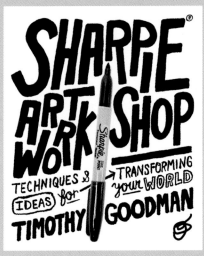

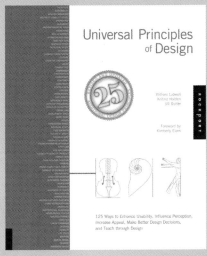